KU-577-406

CONTENTS

WHAT'S IN YOUR GUIDEBOOK?

Independent authors Impartial, up-to-date information from our travel experts who meticulously source local knowledge.

Experience Thomas Cook's 165 years in the travel industry and guidebook publishing enriches every word with expertise you can trust.

Travel know-how Thomas Cook has thousands of staff working around the globe, all living and breathing travel.

Editors Travel-publishing professionals, pulling everything together to craft a perfect blend of words, pictures, maps and design.

You, the traveller We deliver a practical, no-nonsense approach to information, geared to how you really use it.

ABOUT THE AUTHOR

Ryan Levitt is a travel writer and editor who has worked for some of the UK's leading magazines, newspapers and publishers including the *Independent on Sunday*, *Wallpaper*, *Arena*, *Jumeirah International*, *Cathay Pacific Inflight*, VisitBritain, the German National Tourist Office and many more. He has also appeared on BBC Radio's *Traveller's Tree* as an expert discussing New York City.

▶ *The splendid Iguaçu Falls*

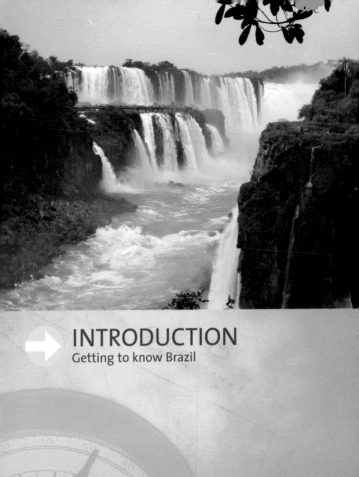

INTRODUCTION
Getting to know Brazil

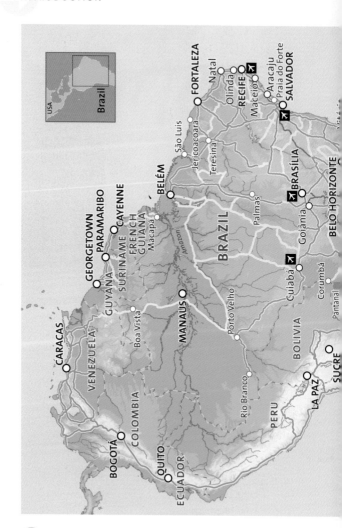

Getting to know Brazil

A land of incredible diversity and a sun-drenched beach destination, Brazil is everything and anything to those who fall for its samba-infused charms. Boasting some of the world's most beautifully situated cities and a welcoming population, South America's largest nation is ripe for exploration by even the most timid of souls.

For most, Rio de Janeiro is the first stop that comes to mind when planning a holiday in Brazil. Ever since Fred Astaire and Ginger Rogers decided to fly down to Rio, the 'Cidade Maravilhosa', or Marvellous City, has been the top destination among global jet-setters drawn to this metropolis of beaches and balmy sunshine. Here you'll find the tall, tanned wonders of Ipanema, bronzed beach volleyball players on Copacabana, and one of the New Seven Wonders of the World, the statue of Christ the Redeemer on Corcovado.

From Rio, the beaches of the south are just a short hop away. Choose the relaxed sophistication of Búzios, formerly the playground of choice for French film star Brigitte Bardot. Or go where Brazilians head when they're looking for a spot of paradise: the city of Florianópolis with its many beaches, one suitable for each personality and day of the week.

To the north lies Bahia state, Brazil's colonial secret-keeper. Salvador is the heart that pumps blood through the soul of this region, known for its amazing seafood, vibrant Afro-Brazilian population, sultry music and unique religious practices. *Candomblé*, which combines elements from West African tribal culture with Roman Catholicism, is a colourful practice featuring highly ritualised ceremonies overseen by a priest. If you can get an invitation to an actual *Candomblé* temple, it is sure to be a highlight of your stay.

Further along the coast to the north is Recife. Recife and nearby Olinda are unique in Brazil, having been ruled over by both the Portuguese and Dutch during their formative years. In Olinda you'll find the first synagogue to be built in the Americas, constructed while the tolerant Dutch were here.

Finally, there are the interior regions of the Amazon and the Pantanal. Spot sloths and toucans or even swim with piranha fish in either the world's largest rainforest or flood plain.

Samba and sun, *caipirinha* and culture... Brazil is waiting for you with its bossa nova beat. When will you move to its sensual rhythm?

🔺 *A surfer on Ipanema beach*

THE BEST OF BRAZIL

TOP 10 ATTRACTIONS

- **Carnaval madness** Join the sambaing crowds through the streets of Rio during this annual party that is regularly ranked as one of the world's most unmissable experiences (see page 41).

- **Witness a *Candomblé* ceremony in Salvador** The fusion of ancient rituals of African slave culture with Roman Catholicism produces this unique hybrid (see page 25).

- **Explore the deepest Amazon** Motor your way up the Amazon either by popping on to one of the regular commuter services or by joining a pre-existing cruise or tour (see page 62).

- **Help save the turtles** Praia do Forte's Tamar project is but one of the many reasons to visit this special seaside community (see page 75).

- **See the chutes** Forget Niagara! Ignore Victoria! Iguaçu is the most spectacular series of waterfalls on the planet (see pages 55–9).

- **Colonial splendour** Olinda (Recife) and Salvador offer the largest concentration of historic buildings (see pages 18 and 25) in Brazil. Manaus's opera house was constructed from materials shipped brick by brick up the Amazon from Europe (see page 64).

- **The perfect beach** Find the ultimate stretch of sand on Florianópolis, the holiday destination of choice for Brazilians (see pages 49–51).

- **On top of the world** Go up the Corcovado, take a cable car to the top of Sugarloaf, or take part in a tandem hang-glide for views over Rio, the 'Marvellous City' (see pages 43, 46 and 104).

- **More modernism** Stop over in Brazil's specially constructed capital, Brasilia. The works of famed Brazilian architects are sure to inspire (see page 87).

- **Size is everything** Walk down the main street of one of the world's largest cities, such as São Paulo, and witness the collision of cultures and classes (see pages 69–72).

🔽 *Aerial view of Botafogo district of Rio*

SYMBOLS KEY

The following symbols are used throughout this book:

ⓐ address ⓣ telephone ⓦ website address ⓔ email
ⓛ opening times ⓘ important

The following symbols are used on the maps:

Ⓜ metro stop   ○ city
ⓘ information office   ○ large town
✉ post office   ○ small town
🛍 shopping   ■ POI (point of interest)
🛫 airport   ═ motorway
➕ hospital   — main road
⟳ police station   — minor road
🚌 bus station   — railway
🚆 railway station
✝ church
❶ numbers denote featured cafés, restaurants & evening venues

RESTAURANT CATEGORIES
The symbol after the name of each restaurant listed in this guide
indicates the price of a main course for one person:
£ = up to R$20   ££ = R$20–R$40   £££ = over R$40

▶ *Prainha beach is a great place to relax*

12

RESORTS
Places under the sun

Belém

At the point where the Amazon meets the sea lies this city, one of the oldest in Brazil. Founded in 1616, Belém was created in order to protect the empire. By holding the mouth of the Amazon, the Portuguese could prevent territorial exploration into the interior by competing nations and hold on to their vast Amazon territory.

The city didn't become economically strategic until more than two centuries after its founding, following the development of vulcanised rubber. As demand peaked, city coffers expanded, resulting in the construction of such follies as an opera house of Italian design using Italian building materials, and a cast-iron market hall shipped from Scotland. After rubber prices crashed, the city sank with them and has never truly recovered. Today, it survives on the tourist radar as the gateway to the Amazon and explorations of the region it was originally founded to protect.

THINGS TO SEE & DO

Forte do Belém (Belém Fort)
This historic fort boasts wonderful views. An on-site museum tells the story of Amazonian tribes and colonial settlement.
ⓐ Praça Frei Caetano Brandão 117 ❶ 091 4009 8828 ⓛ 10.00–18.00 Tues–Fri, 10.00–20.00 Sat & Sun, closed Mon ❶ Admission charge

Icoaraci
About 18 km (11 miles) from Belém, the town of Icoaraci is a popular day trip. It is famous for its artisan shops and indigenous pottery. The main street for workshops is Travessa Soledade, where you can watch pottery being made as well as buy the end product.

Mangal das Garças
This addition to Belém's cultural scene is a large park detailing the cultural traditions, wildlife and vegetation of the region, including lagoons presenting the Amazonian ecosystem.

ⓐ Praça Carneiro da Rocha ⓣ 091 3242 5052 ⓛ 10.00–18.00
Tues–Sun, closed Mon ⓘ Admission charge

Mercado do Ver-o-Peso (Ver-o-Peso Market)

See the Amazon on display at this fantastic market filled with produce,
fish, crafts, clothes and more. The sheer variety of bizarre Amazonian
fruits and riverlife could fill a roll of film.
ⓐ Avenida Castilhos França ⓛ 05.00–14.00 daily

Museu do Círio (Círio Museum)

Belém's most important religious procession occurs on the second
Saturday in October. This museum attempts to explain the importance
of the festival through the use of models and photography.
ⓐ Praça Dom Pedro II ⓣ 091 3219 1152 ⓛ 13.00–18.00 Tues–Fri,
09.00–13.00 Sat & Sun, closed Mon ⓘ Admission charge

Museu Emílio Goeldi (Emílio Goeldi Museum)

Founded as an Amazonian research institute in 1866, this collection of
stuffed Amazonian critters will be of interest to those who want to see a
cross-section of native animals.
ⓐ Avenida Magalhães Barate 376 ⓣ 091 3219 3369 ⓛ 09.00–17.00
Tues–Sun, closed Mon ⓘ Admission charge

TAKING A BREAK

Cosanostra Café £ Café by day, bar by night. The venue of choice for
local intellectuals. Live music kicks off every night at 23.00.
ⓐ Travessa Benjamin Constant 1499 ⓣ 091 3241 1068
ⓛ 12.00–01.00 daily

Sorveteria Cairu £ Sample Amazonian ice cream at this shop. Flavours
are derived from the various fruits found in the jungle, most of which
you will never have heard of, but taste delicious. ⓐ Travessa 14 de Março
ⓣ 091 3167 1476 ⓛ 09.00–21.00 daily

AFTER DARK

Restaurants

Trattoria San Gennaro ££ A stylish Italian restaurant serving bountiful portions of homemade pasta and decadent sauces. ⓐ Avenida Wandenkolk 666 ⓣ 091 3241 0019 ⓛ 12–15.30 & 19.00–01.00 Tues–Sat, 19.00–23.00 Sun, closed Mon

Peixada da Terra ££–£££ Regional seafood specialist. The gaudy furnishings may not inspire you, but the food certainly will. ⓐ Avenida Wandenkolk 691 ⓣ 091 3212 9984 ⓛ 10.30–24.00 Tues–Sat, 10.30–15.00 Sun & Mon

Manjar das Garças £££ Enjoy the lunch buffet or à la carte evening menu packed with Brazilian favourites. ⓐ Praça Carneiro da Rocha ⓣ 091 3242 1056 ⓛ 12.00–24.00 Sun, Tues & Wed, 12.00–03.00 Thur–Sat

Bars & clubs

Bar Joilson This is a fantastic place to hear live samba. ⓐ Rua Padre Eutiquio 223 ⓣ 091 3242 8943 ⓛ 19.00–02.00 Thur–Sun

Cervejaria Amazonas Microbrewery and German food served with Amazonian flair. ⓐ Estação das Docas, Rua Castila Franca ⓛ 17.00–02.00 daily

Iguana Live samba and sizzling-hot dancing. ⓐ Avenida Wandenkolk 284 ⓣ 091 3225 1313 ⓛ 22.00–late Fri & Sat ⓘ Admission charge

Mormaço Open-air club at the end of a pier. Don't fall in the river! ⓐ Praça do Arsenal ⓣ 091 9983 4320 ⓛ 22.00–late Sat & Sun ⓘ Admission charge

Roxy The best disco in town. Music is a mix of local and international hits. ⓐ Avenida Senador Lemos 231 ⓣ 091 3224 4514 ⓛ 22.00–late Thur–Sun ⓘ Admission charge

⬥ *Belém street market*

Recife

Recife is actually two locations in one: Recife, the riverside town founded by the Dutch, with a strongly commercial feel; and Olinda, the Portuguese community on a hilltop overlooking the harbour.

The town of Recife proper isn't really worth a visit, as its industrial nature tends to put off even the most intrepid travellers. Instead, a good option is to use Recife as a base from which to explore Olinda with its preserved historic core, declared a UNESCO World Heritage Site in 1982.

Unlike other historic cities in Brazil, Olinda feels very much as if it is still a city in use and not just a museum showpiece. People go about their daily business in the city streets, mothers put their washing on the line, children play football in the lanes.

Of particular interest is the historic synagogue, the first one in all the Americas, which was founded in the 17th century during the religiously tolerant years of Dutch rule.

BEACHES

Boa Viagem

The beaches of Recife proper are quite polluted. Most wanting to enjoy a stay on the sand head out of town to cleaner beaches. Boa Viagem is the best of the bunch within the city limits, but few people actually enter the water here. You can reach the beach by heading south from the old city for about 16 km (10 miles) along Avenida Boa Viagem. Be warned: this beach experiences the most shark attacks in the nation every year.

Pina

The closest beach to the town centre and always crowded, Pina is a popular nightlife and clubbing spot after dark among locals. The beach is located halfway between Boa Viagem and the old town to the south.

Porto de Galinhas

Located 70 km (43 miles) south of Recife, this beach is worth the drive, especially for families with small children. Clear waters and small-scale development mean that couples and families aren't crowded out. There are plenty of small, traditional properties if you want to extend your stay to make your beach break into a long weekend getaway.

Southern beaches

Head a shorter distance south to the beaches of Praia Calhetas, Praia Enseada dos Corais and Praia Gaibu for better swimming without the crowds. Located along the coast 14–18 km (9–11 miles) away from Recife, these beaches offer the best combination of convenience and cleanliness.

THINGS TO SEE & DO

Capela Dourada (Golden Chapel)

The aptly named Capela Dourada is an ostentatious chapel covered in gold. Everything seems to glow in this gilt-drenched house of worship. There's also a small museum of sacred pieces.

ⓐ Rua do Imperador Dom Pedro II 206 ⓣ 081 3224 0530 ⓛ 08.00–11.30 & 14.00–17.00 Mon–Fri, 08.00–11.30 Sat ⓘ Admission charge

Casa da Cultura (House of Culture)

This handicrafts and artisan centre was once the city's prison. You can still see the original numbers of each cell as you shop.

ⓐ Rua Floriano Peixoto ⓣ 081 3224 2850 ⓛ 09.00–18.00 Mon–Sat, 09.00–13.00 Sun

Centro Cultural Judaico de Pernambuco & Kahal Zur Israel Synagogue (Jewish Cultural Centre of Pernambuco)

The first synagogue in the Americas once sat on this spot. The structure you see today is actually a reconstruction built to honour Recife's Jewish community, which flourished under Dutch rule in the 1640s.

When the Dutch left, so did the Jewish people – mostly for New
Amsterdam (now New York).

🅐 Rua do Bom Jesus 197 ☎ 081 3224 2128 🕓 09.00–18.00 Mon–Fri,
15.00–19.00 Sat & Sun ❶ Admission charge

Forte das Cinco Pontas & Museu da Cidade
(Fort of Five Points & City Museum)

It may be called the 'Fort of Five Points', but there are only four at this
fort built by the Portuguese in 1630. Restoration is complete and
wonderfully effective. Inside, there is a city museum that includes
fabulous artefacts from the period of Dutch rule.

🅐 Largo dos Cinco Pontas ☎ 081 3224 8492 🕓 09.00–18.00 Mon–Fri,
13.00–17.00 Sat & Sun ❶ Admission charge

TAKING A BREAK

Empório Meggies £ You can sit at the café or buy takeaway goodies
from this well-stocked deli. 🅐 Rua Domingos Ferreira 3814
☎ 081 3326 9587 🕓 10.00–21.00 Mon–Wed & Sat, 10.00–24.00
Thur & Fri, 10.00–15.00 Sun

Savor de Beijo £ Clean and simple self-service establishment offering
quick and cheap cuisine. You pay per kilogram according to the weight
of food consumed. 🅐 Avenida Conselheiro Aguiar 2994 ☎ 081 3325 0141
🕓 10.00–23.00 daily

Nau dos Navegantes ££–£££ Tasty Portuguese treats served from this
eatery just a stone's throw from the beach. 🅐 Rua dos Navegantes 1706
☎ 081 3465 3869 🕓 12.00–15.00 & 18.00–24.00 daily

Leite £££ Traditional lunch spot dating back to 1882. Go, if only to
experience the olde-worlde atmosphere. 🅐 Praça Joaquim Nabuco 147
☎ 081 3224 7977 🕓 11.30–16.00 Sun–Fri, closed Sat

◆ *A palm-shaded beach south of Recife*

AFTER DARK

Restaurants

Oficina do Sabor £££ For superlative Brazilian gastronomy, don't miss this much-lauded restaurant, located in a stunningly restored building, with jawdropping views of Olinda. If you are not a fan of pumpkin (*jerimum*) prepare to be converted. ⓐ Rua do Amparo 335 ⓣ 081 3429 3331 ⓛ 12.00–16.00 & 18.00–24.00 Tues–Fri, 12.00–01.00 Sat, 12.00–17.00 Sun

Bars & clubs

The place to head for vibrant nightlife is the Rua do Bom Jesus in Recife's historic downtown.

Arsenal do Chopp Buzzy tables outside – or go inside for some reading, conversation and contemplation. ⓐ Praça Artur Oscar 59 ⓣ 081 3224 6259 ⓛ 16.30–02.00 daily

Biruta Bar Live music, killer drinks and an up-for-it crowd make this bar a true local favourite. ⓐ Rua Bem-Te-Vi ⓣ 081 3326 5151 ⓛ 17.00–late Mon–Thur, 12.00–late Fri–Sun

Cuba do Capibaribe Currently Recife's hottest nightclub. Plays the latest and greatest salsa and Latin sounds. ⓐ Paço Alfândega Shopping Centre, Recife Antigo ⓣ 081 3419 7502 ⓛ 22.00–late Thur–Sun ⓘ Admission charge

Downtown Pub Live music danced to until dawn – a great place to meet locals. ⓐ Rua Vigário Tenório 105 ⓣ 081 3424 6317 ⓛ 22.00–late Thur–Sun ⓘ Admission charge

◔ *Church bell tower in Olinda*

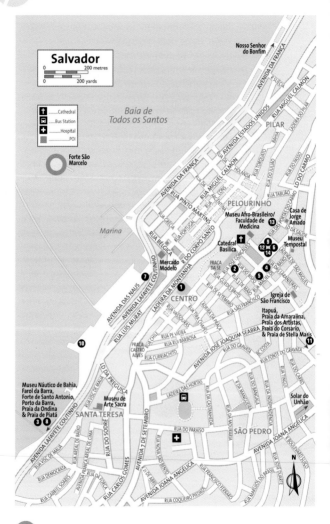

Salvador

0	200 metres
0	200 yards

- 🕇 ....Cathedral
- 🚌 ....Bus Station
- ✚ ....Hospital
- ▪ ....POI

Forte São Marcelo

Baía de Todos os Santos

Nosso Senhor do Bonfim

PILAR

PELOURINHO

Museu Afro-Brasileiro/ Faculdade de Medicina

Casa de Jorge Amado

Catedral Basílica

Museu Tempostal

Igreja de São Francisco

Mercado Modelo

CENTRO

Itapuã, Praia da Amaralina, Praia dos Artistas, Praia do Corsario, & Praia de Stella Maris

Marina

Museu Náutico de Bahia, Farol da Barra, Forte de Santo Antonio, Porto da Barra, Praia da Ondina & Praia de Piatã

Museu de Arte Sacra

SANTA TERESA

SÃO PEDRO

Solar do Unhão

Salvador

Salvador is Brazil's unspoilt jewel. Less visited than Rio and with a much smaller population than São Paulo, it is the nation's eldest sister – the one that hogged the spotlight at first, but has since relinquished its place of prominence to its greedier and more extrovert siblings. Salvador is where African spiritualism and colonial excess ignite to the infectious beat of the samba drums. Buildings constructed in the 16th and 17th centuries litter the landscape and are slowly being restored as foreigners discover Salvador's charms.

Founded in 1501, Salvador is one of Brazil's oldest cities and made its early fortunes in sugar. Portuguese sugar barons created vast plantations in the lands surrounding the city and became very rich – as evidenced by the grand constructions dating back to this period in the neighbourhood of Pelourinho.

One booming tourist trail is the increase in the number of African-Americans who are visiting Salvador, drawn by the city's vibrant, large and significant black population. A massive number of slaves passed through Salvador during the years of transatlantic slave trading, resulting in the development of an important Afro-Brazilian culture in the area. The region even has its own hybrid religion, *Candomblé*. Combining elements of West African tribal customs with Roman Catholicism, it's a fascinating religion with truly colourful practices. If you can snag an invitation to an authentic ceremony, definitely accept it.

If you include Salvador in your Brazilian itinerary, be sure to get out of town at least once. Salvador is the gateway to Brazil's holiday paradise, Bahia. The state is a favourite with holidaying Brazilians because of the laid-back vibe of the region. Don't go expecting quick service and attention to detail. Instead, Bahia is the place to head to for a beachside shack and a cold beer that lasts till sunset.

BEACHES

Bonfim
A popular working-class beach, Bonfim is good for strolls and sports. It is located at the north end of All Saints' Bay.

Farol da Barra
This oceanside beach in Barra is the closest one to central Salvador that is also suitable for swimming. Farol da Barra is located at the southern tip of All Saints' Bay on the side facing the ocean near the lighthouse.

Itapuá
An atmospheric beach community, this beach is the next one along the ocean coast road to the east of Praia de Piatá.

Porto da Barra
Porto da Barra is the closest beach to town. It is located on the bay side of the lighthouse at the southern tip of All Saints' Bay.

Praia da Amaralina
Go here for a great surf and windsurf beach. High waves make it challenging for swimmers. This is the next beach along the ocean coast road to the east of Praia Rio Vermelho/Praia da Ondina.

Praia dos Artistas
This is a favourite family beach because of its gentle waves. Located halfway between the Praia de Piatá and the Praia da Amaralina along the ocean coast road.

Praia do Corsario
The sports beach – come here to join in a volleyball or football match. Situated immediately to the east of Praia dos Artistas along the ocean coast road.

There are plenty of beaches to choose from in Salvador

Praia da Ondina

Shaded by hotel blocks, this beach is popular because of its proximity to some of the large-scale resorts. This is the first beach you will come to after the Barra. It is located on the ocean coastline to the south of the city centre.

Praia de Piatá

This laid-back beach has plenty of kiosks and palm trees. It is located directly east of the city centre; however, you can only reach it by going south along the coast road.

Praia de Stella Maris

Located further than any other beach from the town centre, Stella Maris offers calm spots for swimmers and rougher areas for surfers. This beach is south of the international airport along the ocean coast road.

THINGS TO SEE & DO

Casa de Jorge Amado (Jorge Amado House)

The former home of Brazil's favourite writer, who died in 2001, features a number of texts and photographs that tell the story of his life.
🅰 Largo do Pelourinho 51 ☏ 071 3321 0122 🕐 09.00–18.00 Mon–Sat, closed Sun ❶ Free admission

Catedral Basílica (Basilica)

Built by the Jesuits in 1672, this cathedral benefited from an extensive restoration in 1996. The image of Christ inside is the largest wood sculpture in the country.
🅰 Terreiro de Jesus ☏ 071 3321 4573 🕐 08.00–11.30 & 14.00–17.30 daily
❶ Admission charge

Igreja de São Francisco (St Francis Church)

Built at the peak of Portugal's power, this church is truly the richest in the city in terms of design. The overall result is quite gaudy, but the

100 kg (220 lb) of gold slathered on everything is guaranteed to make a formidable impression. Tuesday between 5 and 6pm is a particularly good time to visit as the city's gilded matriarchs hand out bread to Salvador's poor.

ⓐ Largo Cruzeiro de São Francisco ☎ 071 3321 6968 🕒 08.00–17.30 Mon–Sat, 07.00–17.00 Sun ❶ Admission charge

Mercado Modelo

Once a slave warehouse, this market is now a plentiful source of tourist souvenirs and crafts.

ⓐ Praça Cayru ☎ 071 3243 6543 🕒 08.00–19.00 Mon–Sat, 08.00–12.00 Sun

Museu Afro-Brasileiro & Faculdade de Medicina (Afro-Brazilian Museum & Medical Faculty)

Afro-Brazilian culture and history are chronicled in this fascinating museum. The section on *Candomblé* is of particular interest; you can even find out the location of actual ceremonies.

ⓐ Antiga Faculdade de Medicinia, Terreiro de Jesus ☎ 071 3321 0383 🕒 09.00–17.00 Mon–Fri, closed Sat & Sun ❶ Admission charge

Museu de Arte Sacra (Sacred Art Museum)

Small in size but big on quality, this museum possesses one of the finest collections of sacred art in South America.

ⓐ Rua do Sodré 276 ☎ 071 3243 6310 🕒 11.30–17.30 Mon–Fri, closed Sat & Sun ❶ Admission charge

Museu Náutico da Bahia, Farol da Barra & Forte de Santo Antonio (Nautical Museum of Bahia, Barra Lighthouse & St Anthony's Fort)

This fortress was built by the Portuguese in 1534 to protect Salvador. Inside, you'll find a museum of lighthouse and nautical history and great views over All Saints' Bay.

ⓐ Farol da Barra ☎ 071 3245 0539 🕒 Tues–Sun 09.00–19.00, closed Mon ❶ Admission charge

◔ *The extravagant interior of Igreja de São Francisco (St Francis Church)*

Museu Tempostal (Postcard Museum)

This quirky museum chronicles the history of the lowly postcard. Examples date from as far back as the 1880s and take visitors through to the present day.

ⓐ Rua Gregório dos Matos 33 ⓣ 071 3322 5936 ⓛ 13.00–19.00 Tues–Sun, closed Mon

Nosso Senhor do Bonfim (Our Father of Bonfim)

Salvador's most famous church has gained its reputation from the number of alleged miracles that have taken place following prayer within its walls. Notable features of the church include a painted wooden ceiling and a neoclassical main altarpiece.

ⓐ Largo do Bonfim ⓣ 071 3312 0196 ⓛ 06.30–12.00 & 14.00–18.00 Tues–Sun, closed Mon

Solar do Unhão (Sugar Mill)

This 18th-century sugar mill now houses a modern art museum.

ⓐ Avenida do Contorno 8 ⓣ 071 3329 0660 ⓛ 13.00–19.00 Tues–Sun, closed Mon

TAKING A BREAK

A Cubana £ ❶ Locals love ice cream. Not only is it refreshing: it also appeals to their famously sweet tooth. This place is the best in town.

ⓐ Rua Alfredo de Brito 12, off Ladeira da Montanha ⓣ 071 3321 6162 ⓛ 08.00–22.00 daily

Bahia Café £ ❷ Cocktails and coffees at this bohemian café with views over the bay. ⓐ Mirante dos Aflitos, off Rua José Gonçalves ⓣ 071 3328 1332 ⓛ 05.30–late Tues–Sun, closed Mon

Mercado do Peixe £ ❸ Selection of street food that gets popular in the small hours with post-club munchers. ⓐ Largo da Mariquita ⓛ 11.00–late daily

Sabor dos Saberes £ ❹   Step inside this bookshop to find a cosy café that's good for a contemplative moment of silence. ⓐ Rua das Laranjeiras 5, off Rua José Gonçalves ⓣ 071 3321 6997 ⓛ 11.00–20.00 Mon–Sat, closed Sun

Coliseu ££ ❺   Pay by the kilo at this great buffet restaurant. The wealth of salad selections makes it the perfect choice for veggies. ⓐ Cruzeiro de São Francisco 9, off Rua do Bispo ⓣ 071 3321 5585 ⓛ 11.30–15.00 daily

Jardim das Delicias ££–£££ ❻   Hidden inside an antique shop in a colonial house, this elegant café serves Bahian specialities and also makes for a wonderful venue if all you want is a dessert and coffee. ⓐ Rua João de Deus 12, off Ladeira de São Miguel ⓣ 071 3321 1449 ⓛ 10.00–24.00 daily

AFTER DARK

Restaurants
Amado ££ ❼   Seafood by the waterfront in this beautiful dining room where inventive chefs combine traditional Bahian ingredients with aplomb. ⓐ Avenida Lafayete Coutinho 660 ⓣ 071 3322 3520 ⓛ 12.00–15.00 & 19.00–24.00 Mon–Sat, 12.00–16.00 Sun

Barravento ££–£££ ❽   Dine under the stars at this Bahian restaurant that has a strong leaning towards seafood dishes. Choose an appetiser plate if you're looking for a light meal. ⓐ Avenida Getúlio Vargas 814 ⓣ 071 3247 2577 ⓛ 12.00–24.00 daily

Mama Bahia Salvador ££–£££ ❾   When you're sick of fish, come to this delicious steakhouse serving up large portions of perfectly grilled cuts. ⓐ Rua Alfredo Brito 21, off Rua das Portas do Carmo ⓣ 071 3322 4397 ⓛ 11.00–24.00 daily

Bars & clubs

Bar da Ponta ❿ A modern and chic drinking spot made from glass and chrome. The views at sunset are incredible, and the place has the best wine list in town. ⓐ Praça dos Tupinambas 2, Avenida Contorno ⓣ 071 3326 2211 ⓛ 18.00–01.00 Tues–Sat, closed Mon

Café Cancun ⓫ The hottest nightclub in town for those aged 25 and over. Both Latin hits and Western classics are spun. ⓐ Avenida Otávio Mangabeira 6000, Aeroclube Plaza ⓣ 071 3461 0603 ⓛ 21.00–02.00 Tues–Sat, closed Mon ❶ Admission charge

Cantina da Lua ⓬ Touristy patio with great people-watching on one of Salvador's busiest squares. ⓐ Praça Quinze de Novembro 2, off Rua das Laranjeiras ⓣ 071 322 4041 ⓛ 11.00–late

Habeas Corpus ⓭ A long-time local favourite facing a stage that often showcases live music. ⓐ Avenida Almirante Marquês de Leão 172, off Rua das Portas do Carmo ⓣ 071 3267 4996 ⓛ 17.30–late Tues–Sat, 10.00–late Sun, closed Mon

Quereres ⓮ Brazilian funk in a colonial home. The dance floor is tiny and always packed. ⓐ Rua Frei Vicente 7, off Rua das Laranjeiras ⓣ 071 3321 1616 ⓛ 20.00–02.00 Mon–Sat, 12.00–17.00 Sun ❶ Admission charge

Búzios

The town of Búzios was a sleepy fishing village until French film star Brigitte Bardot declared it her holiday location of choice during the 1960s. Her arrival brought the jetsetters of the day, and the town has been in their sights ever since. No longer sleepy, Búzios is now a popular holiday choice for wealthy Paulistas, Cariocas and Argentinians drawn by the upmarket resorts and exclusive feel. Búzios owes its popularity to its location. More than 20 beaches grace the peninsula on which the town is located – a town that has managed to maintain its romance, with winding, cobblestoned lanes lined with exclusive *pousadas* (Portuguese B&Bs), chic boutiques and restaurants worthy of a Michelin star or two.

Three villages make up what outsiders traditionally know as Búzios: Armação de Búzios, Manguinhos and Ossos. The most historic and prettiest of the bunch is Ossos. Manguinhos is probably the most popular with the masses, and Armação is ideal for foodies because of its great selection of restaurants.

BEACHES

Brava

This is definitely the best beach for surfing. It's located directly to the east of the town centre.

Ferradura

Situated between a pair of rocky outcrops, this beach forms a natural horseshoe shape and the clear waters make it ideal for snorkelling. It's located immediately south of the town.

Geribá

Located over the peninsula from Manguinhos directly to the south, this open-ocean beach is one of the longest in the region. Activity fans love it here, making it perfect for those who want to boogie-board, surf and windsurf.

◔ A boat moored outside Búzios

João Fernandes

Best for people-watching and buzz – this beach is lined with cafés. Located on the land side of the peninsula, it is the place to see and be seen for the in-crowd. It's literally the end of the road to the northeast of town.

Manguinhos

The furthest beach from the old town is this calm stretch of sand that is sheltered from the ocean. As such, it is a popular place for beginner sailing and windsurfing lessons. It's located on the north coast to the west of Búzios town.

Olho de Boi

On the tip of an ecological preserve to the southeast of Praia Brava is this small yet perfectly formed beach. You can reach it by taking a 20-minute walk from Brava. It's often used by naturists.

THINGS TO SEE & DO

Biking

Off-road cycling is available, if a little tame for more experienced riders. Try booking your adventure through **Bike-Tour**.
ⓐ Rua das Pedras 266, loja 4 ⓣ 022 2623 6365 ⓛ 08.00–18.00 daily

Boating

Book a schooner tour for the day and enjoy a trip around Búzios's beaches and offshore islands. Tours include free fresh fruit and unlimited *caipirinha* cocktails. If you want to spend more time at any of the stops, disembark and wait for the next schooner from your company to trundle along. Schooner operators vie for business along Rua das Pedras.

Diving

The best diving near Rio lies about 45 minutes offshore of Búzios. Coral formations are small, but there are good viewings of stingrays and sea turtles available. The **Casamar** dive centre is highly recommended.

ⓐ Rua das Pedras 242 ⓣ 022 9817 6234 ⓦ www.casamar.com.br
ⓛ Hours vary

Golf

Excellent facilities are available at the **Búzios Golf Club & Resort**.
The green fee (around R$90) allows unlimited play for the day.
ⓐ Manguinhos beach ⓣ 022 2629 1240 ⓦ www.buziosgolf.com.br
ⓛ 07.00–18.00 daily

Horse riding

Environmentally friendly horse-riding trips into the rainforest can be
arranged through **Canoar**.
ⓐ Travessa Oscar Lopez 63, loja 02 ⓣ 022 2623 2551 ⓛ 08.00–18.00 daily

Surfing

Ride the waves at Brava beach for small swells close to town or at Geribá
or Tocuns for better crests 5 km (3 miles) from the centre of Búzios.

TAKING A BREAK

Sorvetes Mil Frutas £ Cool down with an ice-cream treat at this stand.
There are literally dozens of flavours to choose from. ⓐ Rua das Pedras
59 ⓣ 022 2623 6436 ⓛ 12.00–late daily

Chez Michou Crêperie ££ Satisfy your sweet or savoury tooth at this
delicious crêpe stand. ⓐ Rua das Pedras 90 ⓣ 022 2623 2169
ⓛ 13.00–late daily

AFTER DARK

Restaurants

Botequim do Baiano £ Pick up a plate of delicious grilled fish or meat
and top it off with a side serving of rice, beans and salad. Yummy!
ⓐ Rua Luis Joaquim Pereira 265 ⓣ 022 9214 0317 ⓛ 11.00–23.00 daily

○ *Búzios offers great snorkelling*

Patio Havana ££ All things Cuban, including cigars and lashings of rum at this seafood emporium which also serves fine steaks, including the local favourite Filet do Partor (steak doused with mustard sauce and stuffed with cheese). ⓐ Rua das Pedras 101 ⓣ 022 2623 2169 ⓛ 18.00–24.00 daily

Shiro Uma Sushi ££ Fantastic sushi using local fish varieties. Fresh and delicious. ⓐ Rua das Pedras 181 ⓣ 022 2623 7445 ⓛ 12.00–23.00 daily

Estancia Don Juan £££ Veggies steer clear – this steakhouse serves only meat. Beef aged to perfection is the speciality of the house. ⓐ Rua das Pedras 178 ⓣ 022 2623 2169 ⓛ 18.00–late daily

Sawasdee £££ Thai food has only recently reached Brazil's shores. You'll find dishes a lot less spicy than you might be used to. ⓐ Avenida José Bento Ribeiro Dantas 500 ⓣ 022 2623 4644 ⓦ www.sawasdee.com.br ⓛ 18.00–24.00 Thur–Tues, closed Wed (Aug–Feb); 18.00–24.00 (Mar–July)

Bars & clubs

Patio Havana More than just a bar, this establishment is also a live music venue, restaurant and chill-out lounge. Seafood is the speciality. Thursday is salsa night. ⓐ Rua das Pedras 101 ⓣ 022 2623 2169 ⓛ 18.00–24.00 daily

Rua das Pedras A street packed with nightlife boasting bars, clubs, eateries and more. Don't even think about arriving before 01.00 at the weekend. ⓐ Rua das Pedras ⓛ Opening times vary; venues stay open until 01.00 Mon–Wed, until 05.00 Thur–Sun

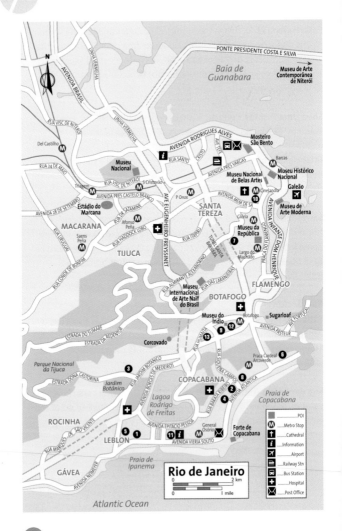

PONTE PRESIDENTE COSTA E SILVA

Baía de
Guanabara

Museu de Arte
Contemporânea
de Niterói

AVENIDA BRASIL

LINHA VERMELHA

LINHA VERMELHA

RUA VISC DE NITERÓI

Del Castilho

RUA 24 DE MAIO

AVENIDA RODRIGUES ALVES

Mosteiro
São Bento

RUA SANTO

CRISTO

AVENIDA PRES VARGAS

Barcas

Museu
Nacional

Museu Nacional
de Belas Artes

Museu Histórico
Nacional

Galeão

AVENIDA PRES CASTELO BRANCO

Thirteen

S Cristovão

P Onze

AVENIDA MEM DE SÁ

Cinelandia

Museu de
Arte Moderna

RUA VISC DE NITERÓI

RUA DR SATAMINI

Estádio do
Maracanã

SANTA
TEREZA

AVENIDA INFANTE DOM HENRIQUE

MACARANA

Afonso
Pena

Gloria

Museu da
República

AVENIDA 28 DE SETEMBRO

RUA URUGUAI

RUA HADDOCK LOBO

Saens
Peña

AVE EUGENHEIRO FREYSSINET

RUA TITIRU

RUA SANTA BÁRBARA

TIJUCA

Largo do
Machado

RUA CONDE DE BONFIM

FLAMENGO

RUA ALMIRANTE ALEXANDRINO

Museu
Internacional
de Arte Naïf
do Brasil

RUA DAS LARANJEIRAS

BOTAFOGO

Museu do
Índio

Botafogo

Sugarloaf

AVENIDA PASTEUR

ESTRADA DO SUMARÉ

ESTRADA DA REDENÇÃO

Corcovado

RUA HUMAITÁ

RUA SOROCABA

RUA VOLUNTÁRIOS DA PÁTRIA

Praça Cardeal
Arcoverde

Parque Nacional
da Tijuca

ESTRADA DONA CASTORINA

AVENIDA BORGES DE MEDEIROS

RUA BARATA RIBEIRO

RUA BARÃO DA TORRE

AVENIDA ATLÂNTICA

COPACABANA

Praia de
Copacabana

Jardim
Botânico

Lagoa
Rodrigo
de Freitas

General
Osório

Forte de
Copacabana

ROCINHA

RUA MARQUÊS DE SÃO VICENTE

AVENIDA EPITÁCIO PESSOA

AVENIDA VIEIRA SOUTO

LEBLON

Praia de
Ipanema

GÁVEA

AVENIDA NIEMEYER

Rio de Janeiro

0   2 km

0   1 mile

Atlantic Ocean

POI
Metro Stop
Cathedral
Information
Airport
Railway Stn
Bus Station
Hospital
Post Office

Rio de Janeiro

When the Portuguese explorer Gaspar de Lemos arrived in Guanabara Bay in 1502, little did he know that he was about to found what is probably the world's most beautiful city. Legend has it that the name Rio de Janeiro – meaning 'River of January' – was given to the city by mistake because its founder mistook the large bay for a river.

Beauty is what Rio is famous for, so much so that it even entranced the royal family of Portugal. When Napoleon threatened Portugal's empire, the entire royal court upped and moved to Rio de Janeiro, making this city the only one in the Americas ever to act as capital of a European empire.

Carnaval is the most popular time to visit. Usually hitting some time between mid-February and early March, it is the world's largest street party. The entire population comes together to battle it out in the *sambódromo* in order to win glory for the various samba schools that perform.

Even if you miss Carnaval, Rio offers plenty of diversions. By day, the beaches are the top attractions, particularly Copacabana and Ipanema. Alternatively, head up Corcovado to the statue of Christ the Redeemer, recently voted one of the New Seven Wonders of the World. Sugarloaf's cable cars also provide spectacular views of the contrasts, both economic and geographic, that have given Rio the unofficial title of the 'Marvellous City'.

Unfortunately for visitors, such glitter also has its dark side. Rio has a huge population living below the poverty line, and large sections of land are covered with makeshift *favelas* (shanty towns) made from scraps of wood and metal. Many of these neighbourhoods are desperately poor and drug gangs are engaged in gun battles with police on a daily basis. Wealthy districts such as Ipanema and Copacabana are situated next to poor neighbourhoods, highlighting the huge gulf between rich and poor.

Rio hasn't been capital of Brazil since 1960, this role having passed to Brasília instead. But the discovery of oil in the Campos Basin has ensured that the city remains financially strong, a fact bolstered by the decision to host the Olympic Games in Rio in 2016 – the first city in South America to have garnered such an honour.

BEACHES

Arpoador

A family favourite, with great surfing. There's also a beach gym popular with bodybuilders. Arpoador is situated on a promontory separating Ipanema and Copacabana.

Botafogo

Don't go to this beach if swimming is what you want to do – the waters are simply too polluted for that. Instead, head here if you're looking for a football match or volleyball game on the sand to join in. Botafogo is located on a bay immediately to the north of Copacabana.

Copacabana

The most famous beach in Rio. The glamour may be long gone, but the Copacabana Palace Hotel still draws the chic and sleek. This famous stretch of sand is located in the southeast of the city, south of Botafogo. Historic military forts stand at both ends of the beach.

Flamengo

Flamengo is a long beach of white sand used primarily by the middle-class residents of the neighbourhood. Pollution levels here are too high for swimming. The beach is located immediately south of Centro and to the north of Botafogo.

Ipanema

The place to go to find that boy or girl from Ipanema you've dreamt of sighing over. It lies to the southwest of Copacabana, separated by the Arpoador promontory.

Leblon

A quiet, family beach attracting moneyed locals from the district. Nestled to the immediate west of Ipanema, Leblon has two lifeguard stations and a scattering of food kiosks.

Leme

Head here for peace and quiet. Rainforest backs on to the beach thanks to its declaration as an ecozone. Situated on a bay to the northeast of Copacabana.

Urca

Good for swimming in the morning, the beach becomes far less attractive in the afternoon when currents push waste on to its shores. This beach is northwest of Leme and lies across the bay from Botafogo.

THINGS TO SEE & DO

Corcovado

Take the train up Corcovado to visit the famous statue of Christ the Redeemer, which was designed by local engineer Heitor da Silva Costa and sculpted by French artist Paul Landowski.

ⓐ Rua Cosme Velho 512 ⓣ 021 2558 1329 ⓦ www.corcovado.com.br
ⓛ 08.30–18.30 daily ⓘ Admission charge

Estádio do Maracanã (Maracanã Stadium)

South America's biggest football stadium is due to host the 2014 World Cup final.

ⓐ Rua Professor Eurico Rabelo ⓣ 021 2568 9962 ⓛ Hours vary

Forte de Copacabana (Copacabana Fort)

This World War I-era fort is preserved as a fascinating example of early 20th-century military history.

ⓐ Praça Coronel Eugênio Franco 1 ⓣ 021 2521 1032 ⓛ 10.00–16.00 Tues–Sun, closed Mon ⓘ Admission charge

Jardim Botânico (Botanical Garden)

Founded almost two centuries ago by Emperor Dom João VI, these botanical gardens boast more than 6,000 species of tropical plants.

ⓐ Rua Jardim Botânico 1008 ⓣ 021 3874 1808 ⓦ www.jbrj.gov.br
ⓛ 08.00–17.00 daily ⓘ Admission charge

◐ The statue of Christ the Redeemer watches over Rio de Janeiro

Museu de Arte Contemporânea de Niterói
(Niterói Museum of Contemporary Art)
Few visit this museum for the works inside. Instead, it's the futuristic Oscar Niemeyer architecture that draws the crowds – and for good reason too.
ⓐ Mirante de Boa Viagem ⓣ 021 2620 2400 ⓦ www.macniteroi.com.br
ⓛ 10.00–18.00 Tues–Sun, closed Mon ⓘ Admission charge

Museu de Arte Moderna (MAM, Museum of Modern Art)
An inspiring modern art museum with arguably the most impressive collection in Latin America.
ⓐ Avenida Infante Dom Henrique 85, Parque do Flamengo ⓣ 021 2240 4944 ⓦ www.mamrio.com.br ⓛ 12.00–18.00 Tues–Fri, 12.00–19.00 Sat & Sun, closed Mon ⓘ Admission charge

Museu Histórico Nacional (Museum of National History)
Brazilian history chronicled from 1500 to today.
ⓐ Praça Marechal Âncora ⓣ 021 2550 9224
ⓦ www.museuhistoriconacional.com.br ⓛ 10.00–17.30 Tues–Fri, 14.00–18.00 Sat & Sun, closed Mon ⓘ Admission charge

Museu do Índio (Museum of Native Indians)
This is a fascinating museum housed in a 19th-century mansion and is probably the finest exposition of native cultures in South America.
ⓐ Rua das Palmeiras 55 ⓣ 021 2286 8899 ⓦ www.museudoindio.org.br
ⓛ 09.00–17.30 Tues–Fri, 13.00–17.00 Sat & Sun, closed Mon
ⓘ Admission charge

Museu Internacional de Arte Naïf do Brasil
(International Museum of Brazilian Primitive Art)
Exquisite art museum with an extensive collection of primitive art.
ⓐ Rua Cosme Velho 561 ⓣ 021 2205 8612 ⓦ www.museunaif.com.br
ⓛ 10.00–18.00 Tues–Fri, 12.00–18.00 Sat & Sun, closed Mon
ⓘ Admission charge

Museu Nacional de Belas Artes (National Museum of Fine Arts)

An excellent collection of 18th- and 19th-century Brazilian and
European masterpieces.

ⓐ Avenida Rio Branco 199 ❶ 021 2240 0068 Ⓦ www.mnba.gov.br
🕐 10.00–18.00 Tues–Fri, 14.00–18.00 Sat & Sun, closed Mon
❶ Admission charge

Sugarloaf Mountain

See Rio spread out below you by taking the cable car up this, the most
famous peak in the city. Cars leave every 30 minutes or whenever there
are enough on board to warrant a departure.

ⓐ Avenida Pasteur 520 ❶ 021 2546 8400 Ⓦ www.bondinho.com.br
🕐 08.00–22.00 daily ❶ Admission charge

TAKING A BREAK

Bibi Sucos £ ❶　No coffee here – instead, the speciality is juice. Tasty snacks
are also available, but it's the freshly squeezed items that should entice.
ⓐ Avenida Ataulfo de Paiva 591 ❶ 021 2259 4298 🕐 08.00–02.00 daily

Cervantes £–££ ❷　The best sandwiches in Rio bar none. Be careful after
dark, as the neighbourhood isn't one of the better ones. ⓐ Rua Barata
Ribeiro 7B ❶ 021 2275 6147 🕐 12.00–04.00 Tues–Thur, 12.00–06.00
Fri & Sat, closed Sun & Mon

Da Graça £–££ ❸　Bohemian, hippie-style café. The colourful junk on
display makes this venue worth a visit. Food is served tapas-style
whereby you can mix and match according to your tastes (much like the
décor itself). ⓐ Rua Pacheco Leão 780 ❶ 021 2249 5484 🕐 12.00–01.00
Tues–Sun, closed Mon

Copa Café ££ ❹　Devour a divine burger at this sleek and chic eatery
that also mixes up a decent *caipirinha* cocktail. ⓐ Avenida Atlântica 3056
❶ 021 2235 2947 🕐 19.00–02.00 Tues–Sun, closed Mon

Garcia & Rodrigues ££–£££ **⑤** Tasty bistro-style cuisine is served at this eatery with an adjoining bakery and café. Grab a glass of wine, a quick coffee or a more filling meal. ⓐ Avenida Ataulfo de Paiva 1251 ① 021 2512 8188 ① 08.00–24.00 Mon–Sat, 08.00–18.00 Sun

AFTER DARK

Restaurants

Shirley £–££ **⑥** Fantastic Spanish-style seafood that draws a massive crowd. Expect queues at weekends. ⓐ Rua Gustavo Sampaio 620 ① 021 2275 1398 ① 11.00–24.00 daily

Aprazível ££ **⑦** The wonderful home of Ana Castilho has been transformed into a delightful restaurant serving outstanding Brazilian dishes. ⓐ Rua Aprazível 62 ① 021 3852 4935 ① 20.00–24.00 Thur, 12.00–24.00 Fri & Sat, 13.00–18.00 Sun

Cipriani £££ **⑧** This branch of the famous Cipriani chain serves up some of the best Italian food in the country. Consistently ranked as one of Rio's finest restaurants. ⓐ Copacabana Palace Hotel, Avenida Atlântica 1702 ① 021 2545 8747 ① 12.30–15.00 & 20.00–01.00 daily

Bars & clubs

Casa da Matriz **⑨** Old school electro, '80s classics, drum 'n' bass – it's all here at this lively multi-room club. ⓐ Rua Henrique de Novaes 107 ① 021 2266 1014 ① 23.00–late Wed–Mon

Club Six **⑩** Hip-hop and funk in a large industrial space. Live acts, with MC and DJ battles adding to the frenzy. ⓐ Rua das Marrecas 38 ① 021 2510 3230 ① 22.30–late Fri & Sat ❶ Admission charge

Lord Jim Pub **⑪** Feel back at home in this mock-English pub complete with British football on the big-screen TV. While this kind of venue seems cheesy on a Spanish Costa, it feels decidedly cool in Rio.

ⓐ Rua Paul Redfern 63 ⓣ 021 2259 3047 ⓦ www.lordjimpub.com.br
ⓛ 18.00–02.30 Mon–Thur, 18.00–04.30 Fri, 13.00–04.30 Sat & Sun

Pista 3 ⑫ Brazilian electro has been creating waves outside the country for a while. Hear it here to get in the groove. ⓐ Rua São João Batista 14 ⓣ 021 2266 1014 ⓦ www.pista3.com.br ⓛ 23.30–late daily ⓘ Admission charge

O Plebeu ⑬ Always packed; try to push your way in to a second-floor balcony table where the patrons are hot and the beer is cold. ⓐ Rua Capitão Salomão 50 ⓣ 021 2286 0699 ⓦ www.oplebeu.com.br ⓛ 08.00–04.00 Mon–Sat, 08.00–21.00 Sun

● *A cable car descending from Sugarloaf Mountain*

Florianópolis

Also known as the Ilha de Santa Caterina, Florianópolis is a dream destination among Brazilians. The area is basically one massive beach. Shorelines are dotted with quaint fishing villages serving up delicious seafood. Powder-white sand greets glittering waves. And all is enjoyed by those in the know eager to keep this treasure to themselves.

The town of Florianópolis itself isn't much to write home about. Instead, you're best to use it as a convenient base from which to explore the area.

The summer months can be hectic when beaches get packed with visiting Brazilians, but pockets of quiet are still available even during this heady time of year. The northeast of the island is always busiest, with the southern region of Campeche offering the most solitude.

For a memorable experience, consider renting a car to take you village-hopping along the coast, where you can sample fish dishes and beach-hop to find your ideal place in the sun.

BEACHES

Praia do Campeche

A wide beach with high waves at the south of the island. Unsuitable for swimming. The beach is on the Atlantic, southeast of Canto da Lagoa or immediately east of the airport across the island.

Praia de Canasvieiras

This great swimming beach at the north of the island offers calm waters. You'll find it situated at the northern end of the 401 road.

Praia da Lagoinha

An intimate and atmospheric beach located between Canasvieras and Praia dos Ingleses. The nearby fishing village offers great dining options, serving up fresh seafood caught that day. Perfect for romantics, it always features some of the best sunset views. This is the very northern tip of the island.

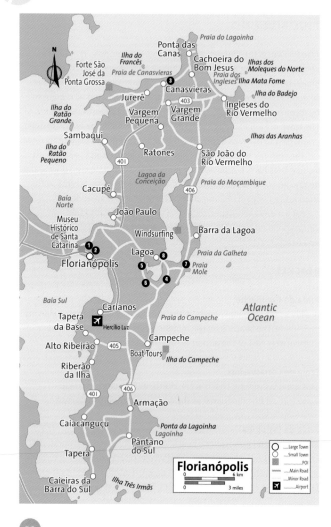

Praia do Lagoinha
Ponta das
Canas
Ilha do
Francês
Cachoeira do
Bom Jesus
Ilhas dos
Moleques do Norte
Forte São
José da
Ponta Grossa
Praia de Canasvieras
Praia dos
Ingleses Ilha Mata Fome
Canasvieras
Jurerê
403
Ilha do Badejo
Ingleses do
Rio Vermelho
Ilha do
Ratão
Grande
Vargem
Pequena
Vargem
Grande
Sambaqui
Ilhas das Aranhas
Ilha do
Ratão
Pequeno
Ratones
São João do
Rio Vermelho
401
Lagoa da
Conceição
Cacupé
Praia do Moçambique
406
Baía
Norte
João Paulo
Museu
Histórico
de Santa
Catarina
Barra da Lagoa
Windsurfing
Lagoa
Praia da Galheta
Florianópolis
Praia
Mole
Baía Sul
Carianos
Atlantic
Ocean
Tapera
da Base
Hercílio Luz
Praia do Campeche
Alto Ribeirão
405
Campeche
Boat Tours
Riberão
da Ilha
Ilha do Campeche
401
406
Armação
Caiacanguçu
Ponta da Lagoinha
Lagoinha
Tapera
Pântano
do Sul
Florianópolis
0   6 km
0   3 miles
Caieiras da
Barra do Sul
Ilha Três Irmãs

○ ....Large Town
○ ....Small Town
■ ....POI
— ....Main Road
— ....Minor Road
✈ ....Airport

Praia da Galheta

Clothing is optional at this beach for naturists. It's located halfway along the Atlantic coast, adjacent to Praia Mole.

Praia dos Ingleses

This is a popular beach situated at the northern end of the island to the southeast of Praia Lagoinha on the Atlantic coast. Because of its location, the beach has a great appeal for activity fans but is less attractive for families.

Praia do Moçambique

This stretch of sand is the longest near Florianópolis. It's designated as an ecopreserve and construction is banned along this area of coastline, so that it is one of the quieter and cleaner options. It's located halfway between the Praia Mole and Praia Ingleses on the Atlantic coast.

Praia Mole

The surf beach of choice for those in the know. Powder-white sand and a backdrop of rolling, green hills bring in the holidaymakers. Located south of Praia da Galheta, equidistant from the northern and southern tips of the island.

THINGS TO SEE & DO

Boat tours

Visit Ilha do Campeche during a boat tour of the eastern side of the island. The tour factors in time on the island to hike, snorkel or swim for a few hours before returning to the departure point. **Scunasul Tours** are well recommended.

ⓐ Avenida Osvaldo Rodrigues Cabral ☏ 048 3225 1806
ⓦ www.scunasul.com.br 🕒 Call for daily departure times
❶ Tour charge

Museu Histórico de Santa Catarina
(Santa Catarina Museum of History)

Formerly the home of the governor, this building now houses a collection of colonial and indigenous treasures.

ⓐ Praça 15 de Novembro 227 ❶ 048 3221 3504 🕒 10.00–18.00 Tues–Fri, 10.00–16.00 Sat & Sun, closed Mon ❶ Admission charge

🔺 *A kite-surfer in Florianópolis*

Riberão da Ilha

Rent a car for the day and follow the SC-405 south to Riberão da Ilha for a pleasant day of coastal exploration. Lining the 401 coast road are colourful villages, originally built by migrant fisherfolk from the Azores. Their descendants still form the basis of these communities. Be sure to factor in a meal at one of the village seafood restaurants for the culinary highlight of your visit.

Windsurfing

Head over to the Lagoa da Conceição to catch a gust and windsurf in the lagoon. Beginners can join one of the eight-hour introductory lessons. More advanced windsurfers can choose instead to rent top-notch equipment. **Open Winds** is a good choice for all your windsurfing needs.

ⓐ Lagoa da Conceição ⓣ 048 3232 5004 ⓛ Hours vary according to season and weather; call on the day to check availability ⓘ Rental charge

TAKING A BREAK

Café des Artes £ ❶ Sandwiches, salads, coffees and cakes are served up to the local bohemian and intellectual crowd here. ⓐ Rua Esteves Júnior 734 ⓣ 048 3322 0690 ⓛ 11.30–23.00 Mon–Sat, closed Sun

Restaurante Natural £ ❷ Veggies will love the great options and cheap prices at this buffet serving everything but meat. ⓐ Rua Visconde de Ouro Preto 298 ⓣ 048 3223 4507 ⓛ 11.00–15.30 Mon–Fri, closed Sat & Sun

AFTER DARK

Restaurants

Bistrô d'Acampora £££ ❸ Home cooking reaches its zenith at this intimate restaurant located within the home of Zeca Acampora. Indulge in superb French-Italian gourmet cooking and muse over the family's extensive art collection. The menu changes frequently according to the

seasons and the wine list is comprehensive. ⓐ Canasvieras km 10
ⓣ 048 3235 1073 ⓛ 20.00–24.00 Tues–Sat, closed Mon

Bistrô Isadora Duncan £££ ❹ Every dish is a love affair in your mouth
and every table a setting for romance and passion. There are only a few
spots to sit at, so book in advance to wow your partner with a night to
remember. ⓐ Rodovia Jornalista Manuel de Menezes 2658 ⓣ 048 3232
7210 ⓦ www.bistroisadoraduncan.com.br ⓛ 18.00–24.00 Mon–Sat,
closed Sun

Pizzaria Basilico £££ ❺ Fantastic pizzeria offering a wide range of
toppings. The only reason why it's so expensive is because each pizza
can feed at least three people. ⓐ Rua Laurindo Januário da Silveira 647
ⓣ 048 3232 1129 ⓛ 19.00–24.00 daily

Villa Magionne £££ ❻ Mediterranean food is done with Brazilian
flair at this intimate house with views of a garden and the lagoon.
Truly delicious food. ⓐ Rua da Amizade 273 ⓣ 048 3232 6859
ⓛ 19.00–01.00 Mon–Fri, 12.00–17.00 & 19.00–01.00 Sat & Sun. Owner
will close on Mondays and Tuesdays when the season is slow. Call ahead
to check confirmed schedules.

Bars & clubs
Latitude 27 ❼ Popular party spot that showcases live local bands.
ⓐ Estrada Geral da Barra da Lagoa 565 ⓣ 048 3234 2420 ⓛ 22.00–late
Thur–Sun, closed Mon–Wed ❶ Admission charge

Mandalla ❽ Sip your drinks as you sway to the music of the nightly
live bands playing Latin and salsa vibes. The views over the lagoon
are inspiring. ⓐ Rodovia Admar Gonzaga 4720 ⓣ 048 3234 8714
ⓛ 22.00–late Tues–Sun, closed Mon

Foz do Iguaçu

There are more than 275 waterfalls making up the UNESCO World Heritage Site that is Iguaçu. First discovered in 1540, the region is now a treasured national park. Vastly larger than North America's Niagara Falls, Iguaçu is rivalled only by Victoria Falls in southern Africa. The falls are located on the border with Argentina, and debate rages as to which side provides the better viewing. The best option is to visit both sides in order to make up your own mind. The border crossing is fairly relaxed, but you should still bring your passport. The area around the falls is a microclimate formed by the mist thrown up by the churning waters. Along the banks lies lush vegetation, and an incredible array of birdlife is to be found here.

Visiting Iguaçu is a challenge. The remote location is what has kept the area so pristine all these years – so you'll have to bank on travelling by air if you want to reach the destination without a lot of hassle. Consider booking your stay as part of a Brazilian air pass that allows you to visit numerous stops in the country during your holiday.

THINGS TO SEE & DO

Cânion Iguaçu
Challenge your stamina by going to this activity centre that allows you to tackle obstacle and ropes courses. Climb, rappel and raft to your heart's content.
ⓐ Parque Nacional do Iguaçu ☎ 045 3529 9175
ⓦ www.campodesafios.com.br ◐ 09.00–17.30 daily ❶ Admission charge

Helisul Helicopter Tours
Taking a helicopter tour is a highlight of any visit to the park, but you do need to consider the ecological damage helicopters inflict before boarding. The noise from the helicopters severely affects local wildlife, with many birds steering clear of the area on active tour days. On the plus side, the views are incredible. The choice is, of course, up to you.

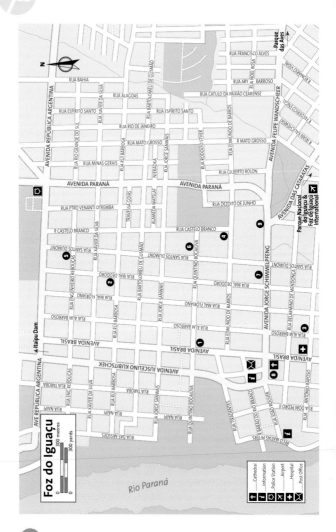

Foz do Iguaçu

Rio Paraná

†	Cathedral
i	Information
⊘	Police Station
✈	Airport
✚	Hospital
✕	Post Office

ⓐ Avenida das Cataratas, Km 16.5 ⓣ 045 3529 7327 ⓦ www.helisul.com
ⓛ 08.00–18.00 daily (Apr–Sept); 10.00–16.00 (Oct–Mar)
ⓘ Admission charge

Itaipu Dam

The world's second largest hydroelectric project spans the border
between Brazil and Paraguay, producing a quarter of Brazil's annual
power supply. Visits must be booked in advance as part of a group tour.
ⓐ Avenida Tancredo Neves 6702 ⓣ 045 3520 6999
ⓦ www.itaipu.gov.br ⓛ Mon–Sat, tours 09.00, 10.00, 14.00 & 15.00

Macuco Boat Safari

Get up close and personal to the falls by joining a boat tour that takes
you to the base of some of the smaller chutes.
ⓐ Parque Nacional do Iguaçu ⓣ 045 3574 4244 ⓦ www.macucosafari.com.br
ⓛ 08.00–17.30 Tues–Sun, closed Mon ⓘ Admission charge

Parque das Aves (Aves Park)

Enjoy some of the best birdwatching in the region by wandering
through the massive aviaries at this 5-hectare (12-acre) site.
ⓐ Rodovia das Cataratas, Km 11, 300 m (984 ft) before the national park
entrance ⓣ 045 3529 8282 ⓦ www.parquedasaves.com.br
ⓛ 08.30–18.00 daily ⓘ Admission charge

Parque Nacional do Iguaçu (Iguaçu National Park – Brazilian side)

Renovations have upgraded the visitors' centre and added a restaurant.
Coaches take you from the centre along the banks.
ⓐ Rodovia das Cataratas, Km 18 ⓣ 045 3572 2261
ⓦ www.cataratasdoiguacu.com.br ⓛ 13.00–18.00 Mon, 08.00–18.00
Tues–Sun ⓘ Admission charge

Parque Nacional Iguazú (Iguazú National Park– Argentinian side)

Depart from the new visitors' centre on the narrow-gauge railway to the
Devil's Throat walkway. The rail journey takes 20 minutes; departures

◆ *The Iguaçu Falls on the border of Brazil and Argentina*

leave from and return to the visitors' centre every half hour. More intrepid visitors can choose to hike the upper or lower trail.

ⓐ Parque Nacional Iguazú ① +54 3757 420 722

ⓦ www.iguazuargentina.com ① 08.00–19.00 daily ① Admission charge

TAKING A BREAK

Marias e Maria Confeitaria £ ❶ Grab a meat- or cheese-stuffed pastry here for a tasty snack on the go. ⓐ Avenida Brasil 505 ① 045 3523 5472 ① 08.00–22.00 daily

NetPub £ ❷ Cheap buffet and internet café all in one. A real backpacker hangout. ⓐ Rua Rui Barbosa 549 ① 045 3572 5773 ① 11.00–15.00 Mon–Fri, closed Sat & Sun

Ver o Verde £ ❸ Cheap and filling vegetarian buffet. Don't go for the atmosphere – just the food. ⓐ Rua Almirante Barroso 1713 ① 045 3574 5647 ① 11.30–15.00 daily

AFTER DARK

Restaurants
Armazém ££ ❹ Intimate eatery serving great Brazilian food in a cosy colonial-era home. ⓐ Rua Edmundo de Barros 446 ① 045 3572 7422 ① 18.00–02.00 daily

Bufalo Branco Churrascaria £££ ❺ Grilled meat – or *churrasco*, as it is known locally – is Brazil's favourite meal. Load up at this fixed-price establishment and choose from a range of delicious grilled meats, fish and chicken. ⓐ Rua Engenheiro Rebouças 530 ① 045 3523 9744 ⓦ www.bufalobranco.com.br ① 11.00–23.00 daily

Zaragoza £££ ❻ Finally! Something other than buffet food or Brazilian. Spanish cuisine is what's on the menu here, and seafood options are

particularly strong. ⓐ Rua Quintino Bocaiúva 882 ⓣ 045 3574 3084
ⓦ www.restaurantezaragoza.com.br ⓛ 11.30–15.00 & 19.00–24.00 daily

Bars & clubs

Bar do Capitão ❼   A lively bar with a pleasant outdoor patio.
ⓐ Avenida Jorge Schimmelpfeng 288, off Rua Mal Deodoro
ⓣ 045 3572 1512 ⓛ 18.00–01.00 daily

Cachaçaria Água Doce ❽   Fantastic mojitos and other cocktails using
local *cachaça* rum as a base. Deceptively potent! ⓐ Rua Benjamin
Constant 63, beside the cathedral ⓣ 045 3523 7715 ⓛ 18.00–late

Tass Bier and Club ❾   At the epicentre of Foz's nightlife scene, this
buzzing bar attracts an ebullient mix of locals and tourists who spill out
on to the large patio. It is mostly a beer drinker's type of place but you'll
also encounter cocktail drinkers glitzed up for the night. ⓐ Avenida
Jorge Schimmelpfeng 450 ⓣ 045 3523 5373 ⓛ 18.00–01.30 daily
❶ Admission charge

🔺 *A toucan in the Iguaçu park*

Manaus

The city of Manaus truly shouldn't exist. Cut off from the rest of Brazil by dense rainforest and inaccessible by road for much of the year, it is a miraculous place and the largest centre in the Amazon. More than 1.6 million people call Manaus home, eking out a living in a city that was once one of the richest on the planet.

At the end of the 19th century, Manaus experienced a financial boom as a result of the huge demand for rubber. It was during this period that the majority of the city's most notable sights were built, including the glittering Teatro Amazonas complete with marble shipped slab by slab from Italy and tons of gold gilt.

The rubber boom died out just three decades after it began, but interest in Amazonian culture and ecotourism has brought a new influx of visitors into the city.

THINGS TO SEE & DO

Centro Cultural Palácio Rio Negro (Rio Negro Cultural Centre)
Once the palatial home of a German rubber baron, this gorgeous building now houses a number of cultural institutions and museums. There is also a good café onsite.
ⓐ Avenida 7 de Setembro 1540 ❶ 092 3232 4450
🕐 10.00–17.00 Tues–Fri, 14.00–18.00 Sat & Sun, closed Mon

CIGS Zoo
There's a wide collection of local animals here; some enclosures are cutting-edge, others depressingly small.
ⓐ Estrada do Ponta Negra, Km 13 ❶ 092 3625 2044 🕐 09.00–16.30 Tues–Sun, closed Mon ❶ Admission charge

Encontro da Aguas (Meeting of the Waters)
The point where the inky, slow waters of the Rio Negro meet the muddy, brown, faster waters of the Rio Solimões has been a major

tourist attraction for more than two centuries. Keep an eye open for the famous pink dolphins.

❶ Day tours available through numerous operators.
Check with your hotel concierge for details.

Mercado Adolpho Lisboa (Adolpho Lisboa Market)

Wander around the stalls to see a dazzling array of fish, vegetables and other everyday local edibles.

ⓐ Rua dos Barés 46 **❶** 092 3233 0469 **⒧** 06.00–18.00 Mon–Sat, 06.00–12.00 Sun

---

AMAZON GUIDE

The Amazon rainforest

This is the richest and most diverse region in the world. Every tree supports more than 40 insect species and there are over 2,000 species of fish in the Amazon River alone. It is the largest tropical rainforest on the planet, with water levels rising to a peak in March and April, when the riverbanks are frequently broken.

Cruising the Amazon

Numerous boats ply the waters of the Amazon in conditions suiting all budgets and requirements. The cheapest cruises are on the ferries that transport locals up and down the river. Don't expect any comforts or viewing opportunities if you take this option. If you want to take a photo, you'll have to work around the boat schedules and the volume of people on board. For something more upmarket, consider the three- and four-day cruises offered by companies such as **Amazon Clipper Cruises** (**ⓦ** www.amazonclipper.com.br).

Lodge holidays

There are a number of lodges of varying quality within a three-hour journey of Manaus. Lodge holidays usually include a nature hike, caiman and pink dolphin spotting, piranha fishing and visits to local native villages.

◔ The Amazon River near Manaus

Museu do Índio (Museum of Native Indians)

Artefacts, displays, photos and models tell the story of the indigenous peoples of the Upper Rio Negro.

a Rua Duque de Caxias 356 **t** 092 3635 1922 **l** 08.30–11.30 & 14.00–16.00 Mon–Fri, 08.30–11.30 Sat, closed Sun

Teatro Amazonas (Amazon Theatre)

Built in 1896 during the heady peak of the rubber boom, this opera house is a glittering jewel, now rarely hosting performances.

a Praça São Sebastião **t** 092 3622 1880 **l** 09.00–16.00 Mon–Sat, closed Sun **!** Admission charge

TAKING A BREAK

Bar do Armando £ The place to go when you need a break from the non-stop Brazilian party. **a** Rua 10 de Julho 593 **l** 12.00–24.00 Mon–Sat, closed Sun

Filosóphicus £ The only veggie place in town. Meals are served buffet-style and priced according to weight. **a** Avenida Sete de Setembro 752, 3rd floor **t** 092 3234 2224 **l** 11.00–14.30 Mon–Fri, closed Sat & Sun

Glacial Sorveteria £ Ice cream made from exotic Amazonian fruit flavours. **a** Avenida Getúlio Vargas 161 **t** 092 3233 4172 **l** 08.00–23.00 Mon–Thur, 08.00–23.30 Fri–Sun

Skina dos Sucos £ Cool down with a refreshing glass of juice made from one of a dozen exotic Amazonian fruit flavours. **a** Avenida Eduardo Ribeiro at Rua 24 de Maio **t** 092 3233 1970 **l** 07.00–19.45 Mon–Fri, 07.00–19.00 Sat, closed Sun

◆ *Steps wind up to the Teatro Amazonas (Amazon Theatre)*

AFTER DARK

Restaurants
Fiorentina £–££ Sick of fish yet? Then head to this Italian eatery that serves up the best pizza and pasta in the area. Sundays offer a well-priced, all-you-can-eat buffet. ⓐ Praça da Polícia ⓣ 092 3232 1295 ⓛ 11.00–15.00 & 18.00–22.30 Mon–Fri, 11.30–15.00 & 18.00–22.00 Sat & Sun

Choppicanha Bar & Grill ££ A typical Brazilian grill in an atypical location – on a pier overlooking the Amazon River. ⓐ Rua Marquês de Santa Cruz 25 ⓣ 092 3631 1111 ⓛ 11.00–15.00 & 18.00–23.30 Mon–Sat, 11.00–16.00 Sun

Bars & clubs
Coração Blue Popular nightspot with a different music and dance theme each evening. ⓐ Estrada de Ponta Negra ⓣ 092 3658 4057 ⓛ 21.00–late Mon–Sat, closed Sun ⓘ Admission charge

Enigma Gays, straights and everything in between come to this sizzling club to dance till dawn. ⓐ Rua Silva Ramos 1054 ⓣ 092 3234 7985 ⓛ 23.00–late Thur–Sat, closed Sun–Wed ⓘ Admission charge

Laranjinha Bar The best place for people-watching in Ponta Negra. Too bad about the tacky floor shows. ⓐ On the waterfront, Ponta Negra ⓣ 092 3658 5483 ⓛ 17.00–03.00 Mon–Sat, 17.00–05.00 Sun

● *The brilliant blue hyacinth macaw in The Pantanal*

 EXCURSIONS
Out & about

EXCURSIONS

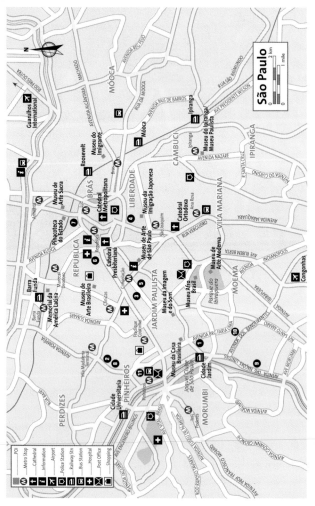

São Paulo
0   2 km
0   1 mile

São Paulo

Rio might have the beaches, but São Paulo has the money. This is one of Brazil's largest cities – and the gateway that most international visitors stop at first. Despite this, few get off the plane to spend time in the megalopolis, turned off by the vast sprawl of *favelas* that surrounds the city right up to the fencing that encircles the airport. However, to ignore São Paulo is to miss out on a metropolis packed with amazing sights and culture, including some of the best Japanese cuisine in the world thanks to the large population of Japanese that call the city home.

GETTING THERE

From other cities, São Paulo is the best-connected metropolitan area in Brazil, with buses, low-cost flights and trains linking to almost every corner of the country.

THINGS TO SEE & DO

Memorial da América Latina (Monument to Latin America)

Designed by Oscar Niemeyer, this monument holds art and other exhibits from across Latin America.

ⓐ Avenida Auro Soares de Moura Andrade 664 ⓣ 011 3823 4600
ⓦ www.memorial.org.br ⓛ 09.00–18.00 Tues–Sun, closed Mon

Museu Afro Brasil (Afro-Brazilian Museum)

One of São Paulo's recent cultural additions, this museum takes a look at Brazil's large and vibrant African population. History, culture, art and achievement are all examined.

ⓐ Parque do Ibirapuera ⓣ 011 5579 0593 ⓦ www.museuafrobrasil.com.br
ⓛ 10.00–18.00 Tues–Sun, closed Mon ⓘ Free admission

Museu de Arte Brasileira (Museum of Brazilian Art)

Despite its name, this museum is actually dedicated to large, frequently changing exhibitions of international artists.

Ⓐ Rua Alagoas 903 Ⓣ 011 3662 7198 Ⓦ www.faap/br/museu/museu.htm
Ⓛ 10.00–21.00 Tues–Fri, 10.00–18.00 Sat & Sun, closed Mon
Ⓘ Free admission

Museu de Arte Moderna (MAM, Museum of Modern Art)

This venue hosts a constantly changing collection of modern art –
usually focusing on the work of a particular artist.
Ⓐ Parque do Ibirapuera Ⓣ 011 5549 9688 Ⓦ www.mam.org.br
Ⓛ 10.00–18.00 Tues–Sun, closed Mon Ⓘ Admission charge

Museu de Arte Sacra (Museum of Sacred Art)

A former monastery, this museum houses a beautiful collection of
sacred Catholic artefacts including chalices, crosses and statues.
Ⓐ Avenida Tiradentes 676 Ⓣ 011 3326 5393 Ⓛ 11.00–18.00 Tues–Fri,
10.00–18.00 Sat & Sun, closed Mon Ⓘ Admission charge

Museu de Arte de São Paulo (MASP, São Paulo Museum of Art)

Brazil's finest art collection is at this museum. Boasting a wealth
of masterpieces from the Renaissance to the Impressionists and
everything in between, including Edgar Degas' complete sculpture
collection, it is now spending most of its funds and focus on building
its collection of Brazilian work.
Ⓐ Avenida Paulista 1578 Ⓣ 011 3251 5644 Ⓦ www.masp.art.br
Ⓛ 11.00–18.00 Tues–Sun, closed Mon Ⓘ Admission charge

Museu da Casa Brasileira (Brazilian House Museum)

Once the home of a leading Brazilian society family, this neoclassical-
style villa now celebrates the decorative arts in the form of the
paintings, furniture, porcelain, silver and other objects collected
by the owners.
Ⓐ Avenida Brigadeiro Faria Lima 2705 Ⓣ 011 3032 3727
Ⓦ www.mcb.sp.gov.br Ⓛ 13.00–18.00 Tues–Sun, closed Mon
Ⓘ Admission charge

● *São Paulo in the morning*

Museu da Imagem e do Som (Museum of Image and Sound)

Contemporary image and sound work created by Brazilian artists offer an intriguing insight into the culture.

ⓐ Avenida Europa 158 ⓣ 011 3062 9197 ⓦ www.mis.sp.gov.br
ⓛ 14.00–20.00 Tues–Sun, closed Mon

Museu da Imigração Japonesa (Museum of Japanese Immigration)

The first Japanese immigrants arrived in Brazil from Kobe in 1908. Today, São Paulo has one of the largest Japanese populations outside Japan. Find out more at this intriguing museum.

ⓐ Rua São Joaquim 381 ⓣ 011 3279 5465 ⓛ 13.30–17.30 Tues–Sun, closed Mon ❶ Admission charge

Museu do Imigrante (Museum of Immigrants)

More than 3 million immigrants passed through this building on their way to new lives in Brazil. Follow their experience through the process.

ⓐ Rua Visconde de Parnaiba 1316 ⓣ 011 6693 0917
ⓦ www.memorialdoimigrante.org.br ⓛ 10.00–17.00 Tues–Sun, closed Mon ❶ Admission charge

Museu do Ipiranga & Museu Paulista (Ipiranga Museum & Museum of São Paulo)

This neoclassical palace now houses an incredible collection of Brazilian art. It was near the site of this building, close to the shore of the Ipiranga river, that independence was declared by Dom Pedro in 1822.

ⓐ Praça da Independencia ⓣ 011 2065 8000 ⓦ www.mp.usp.br
ⓛ 09.00–16.45 Tues–Sun, closed Mon ❶ Admission charge

Parque do Ibirapuera (Ibirapuera Park)

The city's favourite green space holds numerous museums and is beloved by locals. Visit the galleries for culture or use the trails for a jog, a cycle ride or a spot of people-watching.

ⓐ Parque do Ibirapuera ⓣ 011 5045 5177 ⓛ 05.00–24.00 daily

Pinacoteca do Estado (State Art Gallery)
This beautiful art gallery showcases the works of Brazilian artists from the 19th century to the present day.
ⓐ Praça da Luz 2 ❶ 011 3229 9844 Ⓦ www.pinacoteca.org.br
🕙 10.00–18.00 Tues–Sun, closed Mon ❶ Admission charge

TAKING A BREAK

Casa do Padeiro £ ❶ Open 24 hours, this café serves up coffee and snacks to all and sundry. Go, if only to see who happens to be in.
ⓐ Avenida Brigadeiro Faria Lima 2776 ❶ 011 3812 1233 🕙 24 hours

Deliparis £ ❷ Grab a loaf to go, or sit down for a chat over pastries and coffee. ⓐ Rua Harmonia 484, off Avenida Pompéia ❶ 011 3816 5911
🕙 07.00–22.00 daily

Offellê £ ❸ Scrumptious Italian gelato. The chocolate flavours are particularly delicious. ⓐ Alameda Lorena 1784, close to Consolação Metro ❶ 011 3088 8127 🕙 13.00–23.00 daily

AFTER DARK

Restaurants
Kabura ££ ❹ Late-night sushi and tempura done very well.
ⓐ Rua Galvão Bueno 54, near the police station ❶ 011 3277 2918
🕙 19.00–02.00 Mon–Sat, closed Sun

Capim Santo £££ ❺ Bahian-style Brazilian cuisine served in a garden setting.
ⓐ Rua Ministro Rocha Azevedo 471 ❶ 011 3068 8486 🕙 12.00–15.00 & 19.00–24.00 Tues–Fri, 12.30–16.30 & 20.00–01.00 Sat, 12.30–17.00 Sun, closed Mon

Veridiana £££ ❻ It may be pizza, but it's served up in one of the most elegant locations in the city. Traditional thin crust to suit the traditional

surroundings. ⓐ Rua da Veridiana 661, near the hospital ⓣ 011 3120 5050
ⓛ 18.00–00.30 Sun–Thur, 18.00–01.30 Fri & Sat

Bars & clubs

Bar Brahma ❼ The drinking spot of choice for politicians and
intellectuals – just as it has been since it was opened in 1948.
ⓐ Avenida São João 677, close to Pinacoteca do Estado ⓣ 011 3333 8855
ⓛ 11.00–02.00 daily

Fidel ❽ Cool cigar bar with a revolutionary edge. Draws both
high heels and low-lifes – in a good way. ⓐ Rua Girassol 398, off Avenida
Pompéia ⓣ 011 3812 4225 ⓛ 17.30–01.30 Tues–Thur, 17.30–03.00 Fri & Sat,
closed Sun & Mon

Lotus ❾ So cool, it even has its own heliport. Bring a massive wallet
and wear plenty of designer threads. ⓐ Avenida das Nações Unidas 12551,
2nd floor ⓣ 011 3043 7130 ⓛ 23.00–04.00 Wed, Fri & Sat
❶ Admission charge

Mondo ❿ Unlike most clubs in the city, this one draws an older crowd
– so you won't feel like you're partying with babies. ⓐ Avenida Doutor
Cardoso de Melo 1261, off Avenida dos Bandeirantes ⓣ 011 3045 0303
ⓛ 23.30–05.00 Tues–Sat, closed Sun & Mon ❶ Admission charge

Pirajá ⓫ Casual yet cool drinking spot for a long cool one and a natter.
ⓐ Avenida Brigadeiro Faria Lima 64, close to bus station ⓣ 011 3815 6881
ⓛ 17.00–02.00 Mon–Fri, 12.00–02.00 Sat & Sun

Praia do Forte

Once a sleepy fishing village, Praia do Forte is now one of Brazil's fastest-growing resorts. Some argue that the development is resulting in the loss of Praia do Forte's inherent charm, but the decision by many international tour operators to include the destination in their brochures is certainly helping to create numerous employment opportunities. It may be a bit more crowded, but the friendly, relaxed charm still manages to peek through on the streets, lanes and beach strips that make up this sparkling resort.

GETTING THERE

Buses depart daily every 40 minutes between 07.00 and 18.40 from Salvador. The journey time is about 1½ hours.

THINGS TO SEE & DO

Castelo de Garcia d'Ávila (Garcia d'Ávila Castle)

This castle was constructed by the Portuguese in 1552. Restoration is ongoing.

ⓐ Driving out of town, take the road to Salvador for 3 km (2 miles) and follow the signs to the castle ⓣ 071 3676 1073 ⓛ 08.30–18.00 daily ⓘ Admission charge

Projeto Tamar

Until the end of the 1970s, no marine conservation programmes existed in Brazil and sea turtles faced extinction. They were disappearing fast because they were often captured in fishermen's nets, females were killed and nests destroyed on the beaches. Thirty years on this vital project is still providing a sanctuary for these endangered creatures and the project has released more than 8 million turtles into the wild.

ⓐ Avenida do Farol ⓣ 071 3676 1045 ⓦ www.projetotamar.org.br ⓛ 08.30–18.00 daily ⓘ Admission charge

COSTA DO SAUIPE

Brazil is slowly opening up to the package tourist. Tour operators have discovered the charms of the country as an alternative to the Caribbean and have begun offering holidays in the South American sun as a viable fly-and-flop option. One of the major destinations for package tourists is Sauipe, located 9 km (5½ miles) north of Praia do Forte on the Bahia coast. Here you will find a collection of 4- and 5-star resorts with all sorts of amenities including a championship golf course and watersports facilities. It may not be as authentic as a stay in a colonial home in Salvador, but the region makes for a good introduction to the charms this sun-drenched country has to offer.

TAKING A BREAK

Praia do Forte Beach £ There are dozens of shacks and kiosks that line the beach serving coffees, cold drinks and snacks. Almost all of these establishments have no name or phone. Just pick one you like the look of and order.

Tutti Frutti £ Cool down with a scoop from this popular ice-cream shop serving up both traditional and exotic flavours. ⓐ Alameda do Sol 🕒 11.00–22.00 daily

Shrimp Kiosk £–££ Yummy seafood and fish treats prepared at this beach stand in the Praia do Forte Eco Resort complex. ⓐ Avenida do Farol 🕓 071 3676 4000 🕒 13.00–16.00 daily

◔ *The Tamar Project is helping to save the turtles*

AFTER DARK

Restaurants

Forte Dream ££ This is cooking Bahian style. Dishes are heavy on local produce, and fish are caught fresh each day. ⓐ Alameda de Felicidade ⓣ 071 3676 1265 ⓛ 11.30–15.30 & 19.00–23.00 Tues–Sun, closed Mon

Sobrado da Vila ££ Bahian specialist serving succulent seafood and fish options. ⓐ Alameda do Sol ⓣ 071 3876 1088 ⓛ 19.00–23.00 daily

Goa £££ Guests staying at the Praia do Forte Eco Resort enjoy this excellent buffet restaurant included in the cost of their stay. Outsiders can also book a table to savour the food and atmosphere. ⓐ Avenida do Farol ⓣ 071 3676 4000 ⓛ 19.30–22.00 daily

Bars & clubs

Bar do Souza The meeting place of choice for both locals and visitors. The bar-style grub isn't too bad if you need to sate your appetite. ⓐ Alameda do Sol ⓛ 19.00–24.00 Sun–Thur, 19.00–04.00 Fri & Sat

Coisa e Tal Is it a bakery or a nightclub? It's both actually! By day, it serves up fresh bread. By night, fresh sounds. ⓐ Alameda do Sol ⓛ 09.00–02.00 daily

Iberostar Brasil If you want a formal disco, the nightclub at this all-inclusive venue is a good option. ⓐ Rodovia BA-099, Km 56 ⓣ 071 3876 4200 ⓛ 22.00–late daily

The Pantanal

Ignore the Amazon if Brazilian wildlife is what you're after – the Pantanal has plenty more to tempt the ecotraveller. Here is where you will find the country's largest concentration of native flora and fauna, including many unseen outside of the region. The Pantanal is the world's largest flood plain. Visit during the dry season of May to October and viewing possibilities open up, as animals crowd around the remaining waterholes of the area. Holidays are lodge-based, with quality varying from backpacker-style dorms through to 5-star luxury complexes. Head to the region with a sense of adventure and book yourself on an action-packed tour.

GETTING THERE

To access the Pantanal, fly to Campo Grande or Cuiabá and then either take a coach or arrange a transfer through your host hotel or tour operator. For more information, visit the official tourism website ⓦ www.braziltourism.com

THINGS TO SEE & DO

Bonito

This town on the western edge of Brazil near Belém has reinvented itself as the country's prime ecotourism destination. Bonito's tourism industry is run cooperatively, with all excursions costing the same no matter whom you approach. The number of visitors allowed is extremely limited in order to ensure that quality is maintained and negative environmental impact is minimised. The draw of Bonito lies in its rivers filled with wildlife, including anaconda.

From Campo Grande (see page 80), Bonito is a long four-hour drive to Guia Lopes da Laguna on the BR-060 followed by a drive along the MS-382. Tours to this region can be booked upon arrival or through a local operator in Campo Grande.

Campo Grande

For explorations of the South Pantanal, Campo Grande is the city to head for. While the wildlife viewing is not the most inspiring because of the high volume of cattle ranching, the region offers more comfortable accommodation options and easier access.

Chapada dos Guimarães

A popular side-trip from Cuiabá (see below), this arid park is known for its canyons, red-rock formations and incredible trail hiking. It is a wonderful option for outdoor enthusiasts and campers. Chapada dos Guimarães is located 74 km (46 miles) north of Cuiabá.

Corumbá

Difficult to reach, yet more quintessentially Pantanal than any other location, Corumbá is an isolated destination with fantastic wildlife viewing options. Port fishing is particularly strong, along with ecotourism possibilities such as hiking, boating, night safaris and horse riding. You can get here by coach from any major city in the Pantanal or from São Paulo – a very long trip.

Cuiabá

As the capital of the state of Mato Grosso, Cuiabá is the gateway to the North Pantanal and Brazil's ranching lands. There are few sights to see, but the city is a good stop-off point from which to arrange tours and explorations with any of the numerous operators in town. Native craft shopping is popular here, as are 'Western wear' purchases, such as saddles, cowboy boots and hats.

TAKING A BREAK

Amigão ££ Fill up at this buffet where you pay by the kilo – perfect for a lunch that will keep you going through the day. ⓐ Avenida Getúlio Vargas 1235, Cuiabá ⓣ 065 3624 2104 ⓛ 11.00–14.00 Mon–Fri, closed Sat & Sun

⬤ *A wild horse is chased in the Pantanal*

Paraty

This UNESCO World Heritage town is famous for its preserved colonial-era architecture. Prominent during the 1800s, when its port became the main link for the gold mines of Minas Gerais, Paraty faded in importance following the abolition of slavery and the cheap labour it had provided.

Paraty's subsequent loss of population was actually its modern-day saving grace, as the colonial architecture did not need to be tampered with to provide offices or accommodation, and therefore remained intact and authentic. In 1966, the nation realised it had a tourist attraction available and ripe for promotion, and restored the colonial quarter, banning motor vehicles in the process. Since 2003, Paraty has played host to such literary heavyweights as Salman Rushdie and Ian McEwan during its international festival of literature (known as FLIP, see page 108), which, under the watchful eye of founder and local resident Liz Calder (founder of Bloomsbury Publishing) has evolved into a celebration of literature not only for the highbrow set, but also for the local community.

GETTING THERE

Paraty can be reached by bus from Rio de Janeiro 236 km (146 miles). Regular daily departures run throughout the day and take about four hours.

THINGS TO SEE & DO

Casa da Cultura (House of Culture)

This exhibition space and gallery was built from the remains of a former warehouse. Local artists are often profiled.

ⓐ Rua Dona Geralda ⓣ 024 3371 2325 ⓦ www.casadaculturaparaty.org.br
ⓛ 10.00–18.30 Wed–Mon, closed Tues ⓘ Admission charge

Igreja de Matriz (Matriz Church)

Paraty's largest and most ostentatious church. The current neoclassical building was completed in 1873.

ⓐ Praça da Matriz ⓛ 09.00–17.00 daily

Igreja de Santa Rita dos Pardos Libertos (Church of St Rita)

Paraty's oldest and most important church. Built in 1722, it is designed in the baroque style. The building also houses a museum of religious artefacts.
ⓐ Rua Santa Rita ⓛ 10.00–12.00 & 14.00–17.00 Wed–Sun, closed Mon & Tues ❶ Admission charge for museum only

⬥ A charming scene in Paraty after a heavy rainfall

Paraty Tours

Go snorkelling, biking, horse riding and more along the beaches.

🅐 Avenida Roberto Silveira 11 🕿 024 3371 1327 🌐 www.paratytours.com.br
🕐 09.00–20.00 daily ❗ Rental and tour charges

TAKING A BREAK

Arco da Velha £–££ Coffee shop by day, cigar and whisky bar by night.
All in all, a great place to rest your feet. 🅐 Rua Dr Samuel Costa 176
🕿 024 3371 2546 🕐 10.00–20.00 daily

Kontiki ££ Located on Ilha Duas Irmãs, a small private island, ten minutes
by boat from Paraty, Kontiki serves delicious seafood, pasta and
Mediterranean specialities. 🅐 Ilha Duas Irmãs 🕿 022 3371 1666
🕐 10.00–17.30 daily, reservations essential

AFTER DARK

Restaurants
Brik a Brak £££ Regional dishes cooked with pride by the all-female
staff. Live music played on some evenings. 🅐 Rua Dr Samuel Costa 267
🕿 024 3371 1445 🕐 18.00–24.00 daily

Bars & clubs
Bar Coupé Sit down at one of the outside tables to sip a tipple and
enjoy the live music. 🅐 Praça Monsenhor Hélio Pires 197
🕿 024 3371 1283 🕐 08.00–01.00 daily

Café Paraty Technically a restaurant, this establishment goes wild in the
late evening when live Brazilian music is played. 🅐 Rua do Comércio 253
🕿 024 3371 1464 🕐 09.00–24.00 daily

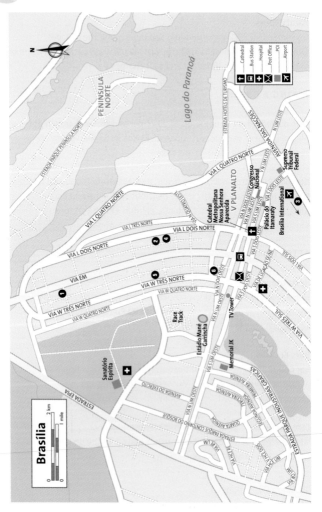

Brasília

Like Canberra and Ottawa, Brasília is often seen as the slightly boring capital of an otherwise dynamic nation. Built during the 1950s, the city was intended to symbolise Brazil's fresh start away from a past of dictatorships, colonialism and corruption. The results continue to inspire architecture fans, with their bold shapes and sheer audacity. Even if you have just a few hours in town, be sure to take a tour to admire modern city planning at its most intriguing.

GETTING THERE

Brasília is in the middle of nowhere and can only be reached easily by plane. Flights crossing the country often change planes here, making it a good stopover location.

THINGS TO SEE & DO

Catedral Metropolitana Nossa Senhora Aparecida (Metropolitan Cathedral of Our Lady of Aparecida)

A white marble and glass cathedral that truly inspires. It was designed by Oscar Niemeyer and only completed in 1970. Long trousers are required to enter the church.

ⓐ Esplanada dos Ministérios ⓣ 061 3224 4073 ⓛ 08.00–17.00 daily

Congresso Nacional (National Congress)

Probably the most famous building in Brasília. This is where the nation is governed from.

ⓐ Esplanada dos Ministérios ⓣ 061 3311 3344 ⓛ 09.30–11.30 & 14.30–16.30 Mon–Fri, 09.30–12.30 Sat & Sun

Memorial JK (JK Memorial)

The founder of Brasília, President Juscelino Kubitschek, is honoured in this memorial that shows scenes of the city being built, including images of the designs that weren't selected.

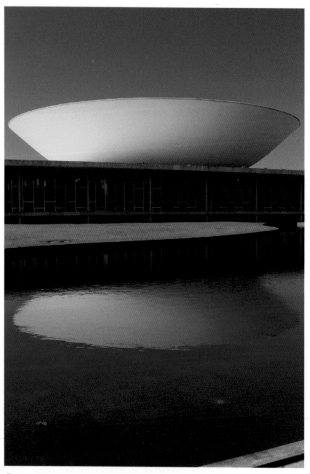

The Congresso Nacional (National Congress) building

ⓐ Eixo Monumental Oeste ⓣ 061 3225 9451 ⓛ 09.00–18.00 Tues–Sun, closed Mon

Palácio do Itamaraty (Itamaraty Palace)

Modernist masterpiece designed by Oscar Niemeyer that now serves as a ceremonial reception hall.

ⓐ Esplanada dos Ministérios ⓣ 061 3411 6161 ⓛ 14.00–16.30 Mon–Fri, 10.00–15.30 Sat & Sun ❶ Free admission

TV Tower

See the city laid out before you from the viewing deck at this tower. Try to go at sunset to really enjoy the panorama.

ⓐ Eixo Monumental ⓣ 061 3325 5735 ⓛ 09.00–18.00 Tues–Sun, 14.00–18.00 Mon ❶ Free admission

TAKING A BREAK

Belini £ ❶ Grab a bite at this combo deli-café that even offers cooking classes. ⓐ SCLS Quadra 113, Bloco D, loja 35, off Via W Trés Norte ⓣ 061 3345 0777 ⓦ www.belini-gastronomia.com.br ⓛ Bakery 10.00–22.00, restaurant 12.00–15.00 & 19.00–24.00 Mon–Sat, 12.00–16.00 Sun

Naturetto £ ❷ The best vegetarian eatery in town. ⓐ SCLS Quadra 405, Bloco A, loja 22, off Via L Dois Norte ⓣ 061 3242 3532 ⓛ 11.30–22.00 Mon–Fri, 11.30–15.30 Sat & Sun

AFTER DARK

Restaurants

Alice ££ ❸ The eponymous hostess serves rich French dishes and superlative wines in the stunning dining room of Alice Mesquita's chi chi abode. No signs are allowed in this district so be sure to plan your journey in advance. ⓐ SH1 Norte Ql.11, Cj. 9. Casa 17 ⓣ 061 3368 1099 ⓛ 20.00–02.00 Fri & Sat ❶ Reservations essential

🔺 *The impressive interior of the Catedral Metropolitana*

Intervalo ££–£££ ❹ The finest Brazilian cuisine in the capital. Daily specials are highly recommended. ⓐ SCLS Quadra 404, Bloco A, loja 27, off Via L Dois Norte ❶ 061 3223 5274 ❷ 12.00–15.30 & 19.00–23.30 Mon–Fri, 12.00–17.00 & 19.00–24.00 Sat, 12.00–17.00 Sun

Bars & clubs

Bar Brasília ❺ A political favourite. Step inside to see what intrigue you overhear. ⓐ SCLS Quadra 506, Bloco A, loja 14, off Via W Trés Norte ❶ 061 3443 4323 ❷ 17.00–02.00 daily

Frei Caneca ❻ Live music club frequented by an older crowd. ⓐ Shopping Brasília, SCN, off Via N Dois Oeste ❶ 061 3244 6711 ❷ 21.00–late Tues–Sun, closed Mon ❶ Admission charge

▶ *Brazil offers great opportunities for swimmers and divers*

LIFESTYLE
The Brazilian way

Food & drink

Visitors to Brazil looking for a fine-dining experience of haute cuisine may be out of luck – in this country, simplicity rules. Ban the fancy sauces! Away with the tiny portions! Brazil is about fresh ingredients and easy preparation. One thing you certainly don't have to worry about is going hungry; that will never happen to you in a country that really enjoys its food.

REGIONAL CUISINE

Immigration patterns, climate and access to ingredients all influence the regional cuisines of Brazil. Bahia's large African population and coastal location give its cuisine a distinct flavour. Meanwhile, German and Italian immigration into the south has created a Brazilian hybrid cuisine that mixes sun with sauerkraut.

The Amazon

Less flavourful than other cuisines, Amazonian meals are based on the traditions of the native peoples of the region. Dishes rely heavily on local starches such as yams, manioc and beans. Locally caught fish is the usual choice for the main dish, with several exotic fruits (many of which you have probably never heard of nor are likely to try again) finishing off the meal as a refreshing dessert.

Bahia & the northeast

Outside Brazil, it is probably the dishes of Bahia that are those most commonly associated with the country simply because they are so distinct. Menu items here rely heavily on the staples of the kitchens of the former sugar plantations, so expect lashings of coconut milk, peppers, and *dendé* oil derived from a variety of palm.

It was this fusion of West African flavours with Brazilian ingredients such as local seafood varieties that was created to appeal to and fulfil the needs of the slave population who toiled in the fields two centuries ago.

items such as *pastel* (stuffed, fried pastry), *esfina* (spiced meat pastry), *empada* (similar to a Cornish pasty, stuffed with a variety of meat or veggie fillings) or *coxinha* (chicken breaded with manioc flour and fried).

Lunch is usually the largest and most important meal of the day. Street food is a popular option for lunch, but be sure to check out preparation methods and storage to ensure you don't pick up any nasty bugs. Alternatively, head to a Brazilian institution, namely the kilo café. Here, you select your meal from a buffet table and are charged by the weight of the food you consume. The heavier the meal, the more you're charged.

Eating out is not common in Brazil, so you will find that many restaurants are aimed at the tourist trade. Sunday evenings are when moneyed families would consider going out, usually to a neighbourhood

⬥ *Caipirinha is a popular cocktail made from sugar-cane rum*

pizzeria for nosh and conversation. Be aware that, when you sit down at a restaurant table, you will usually be served with a small plate of food to nibble on. If you don't want this dish, send it back, as otherwise you will be charged for it.

Vegetarian food

Strict vegetarian food can be difficult to source, especially if you have plans to travel extensively in the Pantanal. Great veggie dishes are available, but are usually served as sides to a meat dish. The best solution is to head for the local kilo café, which usually has plenty of vegetarian options to choose from. If you eat fish, life will be much easier in Bahia and the Amazon, where seafood is a staple. Vegans need to be aware that eggs and cheese may be served in dishes that don't list these ingredients on the menu.

Drinks

Coffee is enjoyed at all hours, and the further south you go the better it is. Most of the finest coffee is exported, so you may find the quality lacking. Tea is caffeine-infused and surprisingly tasty. You are guaranteed a big buzz, especially if you order any made from or with *guaraná*, a deliciously sweet Amazonian berry that has a caffeine-like effect without the jitters.

For something even more refreshing, go to a *casa de sucos*, where locals take fresh fruit varieties of all sorts and blend them with sugar and ice to make tasty slushies. Alternatively, grab a local soft drink made from *guaraná*.

Brazilian beer is usually served very cold in a bottle or on draught. Locals prefer lighter lagers over heavy ales. The best wines of Brazil are produced in the south, but they tend to be sweet varieties.

Finally, the national drink is the *caipirinha*, a cocktail served nationwide made from fresh lime, crushed ice, sugar and a local sugar-cane rum known as *cachaça*. There is a version made using vodka that is often served to tourists, so be sure to point out that you want *cachaça* when ordering.

Menu decoder

LOCAL DISHES

Açai Local berry that is a staple of the Tupi Indians

Acarajé Fried-bean cake stuffed with Bahian shrimp cooked in a coconut milk and tomato sauce

Bobó de camarão Manioc root cooked with the staples of Bahia: coconut milk, peppers, tomatoes and shrimp

Canja Chicken soup with vegetables

Carne del sol Salted, cured beef with beans, kale, rice and squash

Casquinha de siri Crab stuffed with tomato, green pepper, onion, garlic and wine

Cozido Stew, usually with lots of vegetables and a meat of some sort

Farofa The most common side dish in Brazil, consisting of fried manioc, sometimes made with bits of bacon

Feijoada The signature dish of Rio: beef, pork and black beans slow-cooked in a stew and served with *farofa*, kale and rice

Jambú Amazonian herb that causes the mouth to tingle and then numb

Kibe Cracked wheat stuffed with meat and spices and then fried

Moqueca Seafood stew cooked in palm oil and coconut milk

Pão de queijo Tapioca bread stuffed with balls of cheese

Pastel Dough stuffed with meat, cheese or fish and then fried

Pato no tucupí Roast duck cooked in garlic, manioc juice and *jambú*

Picanha Beef cut taken from the rump, served pink and salty

Piranha Meat-eating fish with sharp teeth and bones

Pirarucu ao forno Piranha cooked in lemon juice and herbs

Prato feito Popular lunch plate made from beans, rice, salad and a choice of meat, chicken or fish

Salgados/salgadinhos Fried, savoury snacks
Vatapá Common seafood dish from Bahia made with fresh shrimp, palm oil, coconut milk and tomatoes
Xinxim de galinha Chicken flavoured with garlic, lemon and salt

MEAT & POULTRY
Bife Steak
Carne Meat, in general
Carneiro Lamb
Costeleta Chop
Figado Liver
Frango Chicken
Linguiça Sausage
Pato Duck
Porco Pork

FISH & DAIRY
Atum Tuna
Caranguejo Crab
Lagosta Lobster
Leite Milk
Lula Squid
Ovos Eggs
Queijo Cheese
Siri Small crab

DESSERT
Arroz doce Rice pudding
Bolo Cake
Cocada Baked coconut biscuit
Doce de leite Milk and sugar treat
Goiabada Guava paste
Pavé Creamy cake
Quindim Dessert using egg as a base
Sorvete Ice cream

DRINKS
Agua Water
Cachaça Rum using sugar cane as a base
Café Coffee
Cafezinho Shot of coffee served strong and sweet
Caipirinha Cocktail using *cachaça*, lime, crushed ice and sugar
Cerveja Beer
Chope Draught beer
Erva mate Buzzy tea found in southern Brazil
Guaraná Soft drink made from berries
Refrigerante Soft drink
Suco Juice
Vitamina Juice with milk

Shopping

Brazil has a wealth of local specialities and handicrafts that are sure to do damage to your wallet. From high-end buys such as gems and jewellery to street finds like *art naïf* masterpieces, you will most certainly return home with a treasure of your own.

ARTS & HANDICRAFTS

Every major city in Brazil has a craft or 'hippy' market where local handicrafts can be picked up. If you're looking for top-quality native articles, check out museum gift shops and Funai shops (government-owned shops specialising in local artisan and craft work). Prices are high but match the workmanship put into each item. Craft fairs outside the main centres are usually held at weekends.

BEACHWEAR & CLOTHING

Don't bother bringing any swimwear, as you'll be able to pick up some cheap, hot styles in Brazil for a song – although bikini bottoms are not known as dental floss for nothing! The best buy of all is a pair of Havaiana flip-flops. Popular among the beach set, these casual sandals are *de rigueur* for Brazilians in the know and make a popular souvenir to bring back home. Prices are generally half of what you might pay in Europe or North America.

GEMS

While Minas Gerais is where most gems are mined, the best purchases are made in the jewellery shops of the big cities. Gem scams are rife, so in order to avoid being duped make your purchase in either of the two big gem shops in Brazil: Amsterdam Sauer or H Stern. You won't find any bargains in either shop, but you will be guaranteed quality.

LEATHER

Leather in Brazil is cheap and well crafted but may not be as soft and of the same quality as you might find back home. Leather items on street

⬥ Brazil offers shoppers everything from market stalls to priceless gems

◆ *A typical 'Bahia style' painting*

stalls tend to be made badly and probably won't fit well. Larger sizes are few and far between. For the best quality, reserve your leather purchases for shops and boutiques in high-end shopping centres in Rio and São Paulo. Leather footballs are another good purchase; just deflate them if you want to transport them back home with you on the plane.

MUSIC

For local pop, rock, electro and Brazilian funk, check out the music shops in Rio. Local CDs are about half the cost of what you might pay back home. You can also pick up bootleg mix CDs on stalls across the city. For samba and Bahian music, Salvador offers the best options. Percussion instruments used in native music make for intriguing (if rather bulky) souvenirs to bring back home. Unless you plan on playing them frequently, avoid the high-priced instruments sold in music shops and instead choose something from a street stall geared towards tourists.

LIFESTYLE

Children

Brazilians adore children. You can pretty much bring your child anywhere you go in Brazil, so don't be surprised to find tantrum throwers in fine-dining establishments and small tots playing by a café table in even the earliest hours of the morning.

HEALTH

Nappies are available pretty much across the country, but you might want to stock up if you plan on going into the interior, the Pantanal or the Amazon. Be sure to check medical requirements for any adventurous exploration, as you are advised to get your children vaccinated before arriving in the country.

THINGS TO DO
The Amazon

The Amazon requires a lot of preparation in terms of vaccinations and health, but it also reaps the greatest rewards. Book yourself into a lodge for a few days to experience true peace. Children love the nature walks guided by naturalists and usually thrill to the idea of swimming in waters infested with piranha. As long as your child has no cuts on their body, they'll be fine to paddle. If you can afford it, book into the **Hotel das Cataratas** (W www.hoteldascataratas.com.br – see listing on page 111) where an on-site zoo filled with native animals is waiting to be enjoyed.

Belém

Get back to nature by staying on the nearby island of Marajó. Here, you can work and play on a real buffalo ranch (there are many to choose from) where you can learn horse riding and go birdwatching for hundreds of colourful local species. Check the government's ministry of tourism website W www.braziltour.com for further options.

Foz do Iguaçu

While staring at the falls may be inspiring for you, children appreciate an extra touch of excitement. Book a helicopter tour with **Helisul Helicopter Tours** (see page 55) if your green conscience allows, or a ride on the **Macuco Boat Safari** (see page 57).

Rio de Janeiro

Children love the beach and the views from Corcovado and Sugarloaf. A trip in the cable car up Sugarloaf is always an exciting adventure, while a paddle in the waters of Copacabana or Ipanema is a guaranteed crowd-pleaser. When swimming, keep an eye on your children at all times as the undertow can be strong. Lifeguards have large areas they have to watch over, with many stretches of sand not watched at all.

🔺 *Brazil's beaches offer children hours of fun*

Sports & activities

Brazilians are active people, eager to flex their muscles at every opportunity, and Brazil is a great destination for all sporty types and adventurers looking for rather more than just a camera angle from their holiday.

CLIMBING

Climbing routes vary in difficulty, with many good climbs situated in city centres – especially in Rio. There are more than 350 climbs within an hour's drive from Rio appealing to all ability levels. The best season to consider a climb is between April and October. For more information, try ⓦ www.climbinrio.com

FOOTBALL

No experience quite encapsulates Brazilian culture like a football match. Join the chanting throngs supporting the local team in one of the numerous stadiums. Better yet, try to get a seat in the grandaddy stadium of them all, the **Maracanã** in Rio (ⓐ Rua Professor Eurico Rabelo ⓣ 021 2568 9962 ⓛ Hours vary), which in 1950 hosted the largest crowd to watch a football match anywhere in the world.

HANG-GLIDING

For a truly memorable experience, book yourself on a hang-glide over Rio. Hang-gliding in the city is done in tandem with an experienced professional. Conquer your fears and you'll enjoy some of the most spectacular views possible. ⓦ www.riohanggliding.com

HIKING

Head to the south if you are planning a hiking holiday, especially during the cooler winter months between June and August. National and state parks in this region offer plenty of trails suitable for both casual walkers and more experienced trail challengers. For more details visit the official tourism website (ⓦ www.braziltour.com).

HORSE RIDING

Head to the ranching region of the Pantanal for horse-riding options. Better still, book yourself on a ranching holiday in the centre of Brazil to learn more about rural lifestyles and challenge your horsemanship skills. ⓦ www.inthesaddle.com offers lots of options to choose from.

SURFING & WINDSURFING

While surfing is possible all along the Brazilian coast, the waves in the south have most appeal for real aficionados. Windsurfing is also growing in popularity. Rio de Janeiro and Búzios offer the best surf, usually during the winter months of June, July and August. Hiring surfing equipment can be difficult in Rio, so it's worth bringing boards from home if you're on a dedicated surfing holiday. Búzios offers a wider selection of hire shops. Reasonable lessons and equipment hire for windsurfing are available in Rio and Búzios.

VOLLEYBALL

Beach volleyball is a popular pastime among locals. Brazil consistently vies for Olympic medals in volleyball, making it one of the more popular spectator sports in the country.

🔺 *Volleyball is hugely popular in Brazil*

LIFESTYLE

Festivals & events

JANUARY

Three Kings Festival (6 January) Procession to celebrate the arrival of the Three Kings in Bethlehem. Held every year in Salvador's Praça da Sé.
❶ 071 3321 2463 **Ⓦ** www.bahiatursa.ba.gov.br

Washing of the Steps (3rd Thursday in January) Local women, accompanied by a procession of 800,000 onlookers, wash the steps of Salvador's Nosso Senhor do Bonfim with perfumed water.
❶ 071 3321 2463 **Ⓦ** www.bahiatursa.ba.gov.br

St Sebastian Day (20 January) Rio's main cathedral takes centre stage on the day of the city's patron saint. **❶** 021 2217 7575
Ⓦ www.riodejaneiro-turismo.com.br

FEBRUARY

Celebration of Yemanjá (2 February) Nationwide celebrations honour the goddess of the sea. The largest party takes place on Salvador's Praia Vermelha. **❶** 071 3321 2463 **Ⓦ** www.bahiatursa.ba.gov.br

Carnaval (4–8 March 2011; 17–21 February 2012) Carnaval is Brazil's biggest party, consistently ranked as one of the world's greatest festivals.
❶ 021 2217 7575 **Ⓦ** www.riodejaneiro-turismo.com.br

MARCH

Easter Weekend (dates vary) Processions and ceremonies are held throughout the country. Events in colonial-era churches in Salvador and Rio have a particular beauty.

JUNE

Festas Juninas (13–14 June) This harvest festival is a folk tradition celebrated across the country. Expect music, fireworks and general frivolity.

⬤ *Carnaval is Rio's biggest party*

JULY

Sailing Festival (3rd week in July) This sailing regatta on Ilhabela is the largest of its kind in Brazil. Ⓦ www.ilhabela.com.br

AUGUST

FLIP (varies each year) Paraty's international literary festival.
Ⓦ www.flip.org.br

SEPTEMBER

Independence Day (7 September) The nation celebrates independence from Portugal on this day.

OCTOBER

Círio de Nazaré (2nd Saturday in October) Belém is overtaken by religious fervour as the icon of the Virgin of Nazaré is paraded through city streets watched by up to 1 million devotees. Ⓣ 091 3242 0900

Bienal de São Paulo (dates vary) Latin America's top art event kicks off every other year in Ibirapuera Park. Ⓦ www.bienalsaopaulo.org.br

NOVEMBER

Grand Prix (dates vary) Racing fever grips the nation as the Grand Prix hits the track at Interlagos, outside São Paulo. Ⓦ www.formula1.com

DECEMBER

Santa Barbara (4 December) Celebrating the *Candomblé* goddess of wind, this festival features Bahian dance and music on beaches all over the state. Ⓣ 071 3321 2463 Ⓦ www.bahiatursa.ba.gov.br

New Year's Eve (31 December) More than 2 million people congregate on Copacabana beach to bring in the New Year.
Ⓦ www.riodejaneiro-turismo.com.br

▶ *An angel statue on the island of Ilha Grande near Rio de Janeiro*

PRACTICAL INFORMATION
Tips & advice

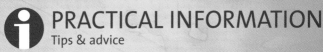

Accommodation

Price rating

The ratings in this book indicate the cost of a single night in a double room for two people: **£** = up to R$200, **££** = R$200–R$335, **£££** = over R$335

BELÉM

Hotel Grão Pará £ The affordable alternative to the Hilton – just two doors away. Rooms are clean and simple. ⓐ Avenida Presidente Vargas 718 ⓣ 091 3224 9600 ⓦ www.hotelgraopara.com.br

RECIFE

Pousada do Amparo £ Atmospheric property made from the combination of two 200-year-old colonial buildings in historic Olinda. ⓐ Rua do Amparo 199 ⓣ 081 3439 174 ⓦ www.pousadadoamparo.com.br

Internacional Palace Hotel ££ Large rooms and a location across the street from Boa Viagem beach give it the thumbs up. ⓐ Avenida Boa Viagem 4070 ⓣ 081 3464 2500 ⓦ www.lucsimhoteis.com.br

SALVADOR

Pousada do Boqueirão £ Step back in time to the colonial era in this stunning inn in the heart of the old town. ⓐ Rua Direita de Santa Antônio 48 ⓣ 071 3241 2262 ⓦ www.pousadaboqueirao.com.br

Pestana Bahia £–££ A massive makeover has transformed this hotel into a glittering jewel. ⓐ Rua Fonte do Boi, Rio Vermelho ⓣ 071 3453 8005 ⓦ www.pestana.com

Pestana Convento do Carmo £££ A wonderful fusion of tradition and modernity make this charming boutique hotel, ideally located in the heart of Pelourinho, hard to beat. Luxurious décor and superlative amenities cater to every whim. ⓐ Rua do Camo 1 ⓣ 071 3327 8400 ⓦ www.pousadas.pt

BÚZIOS

La Bohème £–££ A collection of apartments within walking distance of the village and beaches. ⓐ Praia de João Fernandes, lote 1 ⓣ 022 2623 1744

RIO DE JANEIRO

Ipanema Plaza ££ Enjoy Ipanema for less at this sleek property located just a block from the beach. ⓐ Rua Farme de Amoedo 34 ⓣ 021 3687 2000 ⓦ www.ipanemaplazahotel.com

Fasano £££ Fans of Philippe Starck will be bowled over by this decadent hotel which exudes playful opulence. The swimming pool is simply stunning and makes for fascinating people-watching. ⓐ Avenida Vieira Soulo 88 ⓣ 021 3202 4000 ⓦ www.fasano.com.br

FLORIANÓPOLIS

Pousada da Vigia £–££ Romance lives at this intimate property with just eight rooms – six of which have balconies boasting stunning views of the ocean. ⓐ Rua Cônego Walmor Castro 291, Lagoinha ⓣ 048 3284 1789 ⓦ www.pousadadavigia.com.br

Praia Mole Eco Village £–££ This large hotel offers plenty to keep the little ones occupied. ⓐ Estrada Geral da Barra da Lagoa 2001 ⓣ 048 3239 7500 ⓦ www.praiamole.com.br

FOZ DO IGUAÇU

Hotel das Cataratas £££ The only hotel that is inside the national park. ⓐ Parque Nacional do Iguaçu ⓣ 045 2102 7000 ⓦ www.hoteldascataratas.com.br

MANAUS & AMAZON

Tropical Manaus ££ Massive hotel on the shores of the Rio Negro with a wide range of facilities. ⓐ Avenida Coronel Teixeira 1320 ⓣ 092 701 2670 ⓦ www.tropicalmanaus.com.br

Preparing to go

GETTING THERE
By air

The largest airport with international air links in Brazil is Guarulhos International Airport near São Paulo. Rio de Janeiro is also offered as a destination by international airlines, but most planes touch down in São Paulo first before continuing on to make the additional one-hour journey. **Air France** has a service to Rio via Paris and **Swiss Air** offers flights to Rio via Zurich. **British Airways** fly direct to São Paulo from London Heathrow and **TAM** flies to São Paulo via Frankfurt. From the US there are more options to Rio, including **US Airways** via North Carolina. Charter planes and **TAP Air Portugal** (📞 0845 601 0932 🌐 www.flytap.com) are beginning to offer regional destinations such as Salvador and Recife, so it is worth looking into fares if you plan on doing a lot of exploration in Bahia. The average flying time non-stop to São Paulo from London is 11½ hours, or 9¾ hours from New York.

Prices of flights to South America have always been inflated, but they have become even more steep since the bankruptcy of Brazil's flag carrier Varig in 2006. It is worth being as flexible as possible in terms of scheduling your travel in low or mid-season, as adjustment by a day or two could make a huge difference in price.

If you are planning to travel extensively through Brazil or to enter it from other points in South America, consider flying with one of the new low-cost carriers that serve the country, such as **Gol Airlines** (🌐 www.voegol.com.br).

INSURANCE

Check that your insurance policy covers you adequately for loss of valuables and other possessions, for activities you might want to try – say horse riding or watersports – and for emergency medical and dental treatment, including flights home, if required.

Many people are aware that air travel emits CO_2, which contributes to climate change. You may be interested in the possibility of lessening the environmental impact of your flight through the charity Climate Care, which offsets your CO_2 by funding environmental projects around the world. Visit Ⓦ www.jpmorganclimatecare.com

TOURISM AUTHORITY

Brazil's national tourism agency has offices abroad in both the United States and United Kingdom. There is also a good website offering tips and advice (Ⓦ www.braziltour.com). In countries without a tourist office, you will need to approach the Brazilian embassy or consulate for information.

UK Ⓐ 32 Green Street, London W1K 7AT Ⓣ 020 7399 9100
Ⓦ www.brazil.org.uk Ⓔ tourism@brazil.org.uk
Ⓛ 10.00–13.00 & 14.00–18.00 Mon–Fri

BEFORE YOU LEAVE
Health and prescriptions

It is not generally necessary to take any special health precautions or have any vaccinations before travelling in Brazil. However, if you are planning to travel extensively through the Amazon or Pantanal, precautions do need to be taken. Yellow fever vaccinations are recommended if you are travelling to Amazonia, Goiás or Mato Grosso. Malaria is also prevalent in northern Brazil and the Amazon and you should take a malaria prophylactic if the region is part of your holiday plans. Even with medication, coverage is not guaranteed, and so insect repellent is a must.

Take any regular prescription medicines with you to ensure you don't run out. Pack a small first-aid kit with plasters, antiseptic cream, travel sickness pills, insect repellent and bite-relief creams, upset stomach remedies, painkillers and protective suncreams. Consider a dental check before you go if you are planning an extended stay in Brazil. Once at your destination, you can ask your hotel receptionist or your tour rep to recommend a doctor or dentist in the event of an emergency.

ENTRY FORMALITIES

Visitors to Brazil who are citizens of the UK, the Republic of Ireland and New Zealand will need a passport (valid for at least six months) but not a visa for stays of up to six months, and a return airline ticket. Americans, Canadians and Australians do require visas for all visits, which will allow them to stay for up to 90 days. Applications should be made through your local Brazilian embassy or consulate. Allow at least two weeks for processing. Check the official website for the latest details and customs restrictions (Ⓦ www.turismo.gov.br).

MONEY

The currency in Brazil is the Real (R$). You can withdraw money using ATMs at most Brazilian banks. When changing money, you will need to keep receipts, as you will have to produce them when changing notes back to your own currency before departure. Bureaux de change offer the best rates, but most people choose to change money in banks or at hotel reception desks for safety reasons. The most widely accepted credit cards are Visa and MasterCard. American Express is less commonly accepted.

CLIMATE

Brazil is a massive country, and the climate varies from region to region. In the northeast (Bahia), the temperature remains constant all the year round, at between 28 and 35°C (82 and 95°F). Ocean breezes cool things down a little bit the closer you get to the coast. The winter months of June and July see the greatest amounts of rainfall, but these are usually limited to brief showers in the afternoon that dissipate before very long.

The Amazon is sizzling and humid all through the year, with temperatures in the high 30s°C (around 100°F). Instead of summer and winter, locals have a dry season between June and December and a wet one between January and May.

Rio de Janeiro experiences hot and muggy summers from December to March. The thermometer can go as high as 40°C (104°F) with 100 per cent humidity. Meanwhile, winters can see drops down to 19°C (66°F) at night. São Paulo's weather is the same as Rio's except that its high elevation means that temperatures can drop even further during the winter months.

BAGGAGE ALLOWANCE

Baggage allowances vary according to the airline, destination and class of travel, but 20 kg (44 lb) per person is the norm for luggage that is carried in the hold. You are allowed one item of cabin baggage weighing no more than 5 kg (11 lb), and measuring no more than 46 x 30 x 23 cm (18 x 12 x 9 in). Large items – surfboards, golf clubs and pushchairs – are usually charged as extras and it is worth notifying the airline in advance if you want to bring these. Be sure to limit your carry-on liquids, as you can only bring liquids on board in a small, clear, plastic bag with no more than 100 ml (3½ fl oz) inside.

⬤ *You can enjoy great views of Rio de Janeiro as you fly in*

During your stay

AIRPORTS

The main international gateway into Brazil is São Paulo's **Guarulhos International Airport**. The airport is located about 30 km (18^1/2 miles) northeast of the city. Locals may sometimes refer to it as Cumbica. Even if São Paulo isn't your intended final destination, chances are your flight into the country will land here. Airlines such as British Airways and United Airlines all make a stop at Guarulhos before continuing on to Rio de Janeiro. Domestic flights also use Congonhas Airport to the south of São Paulo. Here is where you will find city hops to Rio and other southern centres.

Aeroporto Galeão, otherwise known as Tom Jobim International, is the airport serving Rio de Janeiro. Few international airlines offer non-stop service to this airport, with TAP Air Portugal being the main exception.

Belém, Belo Horizonte, Fortaleza, Manaus, Recife and Salvador also have scheduled and charter services from North America and Europe, but these will invariably be much less frequent and more expensive. Your choice of operators will also be very restricted.

From all airports, it is advisable to take a taxi to your hotel. Prepaid tickets can be purchased at the airport. From Guarulhos, a prepaid fare will be anything between about R$80 and R$100 depending on what part of São Paulo you are going to. From Galeão, a trip to Rio will cost about R$63.

When you emerge from picking up your luggage, you will be approached by unlicensed drivers asking you where you want to go. Do not hire one of these drivers, as some are unscrupulous, demanding inflated fares. Muggings have even been reported in some cases – definitely not a good way to start your dream holiday.

COMMUNICATIONS
Phones

International SIM cards usually work in Brazil, but the charges are huge – usually about £1 a minute. A better option is to purchase a local SIM card, the charge for which is about a third of that for international calls. TIM (Telecom Italia Mobile) is the only provider with coverage throughout the country, so, if you are planning to travel extensively through Brazil, this is the card to get. Local calls are easy to dial – just ring the number, making sure to drop the prefix area code. Long-distance within Brazil will require you to dial a three-digit prefix and then the eight-digit number.

Public phones tend to be placed at busy intersections. As a result, it can be a challenge hearing anything that is being said down the line. The minimum charge for a local call is R$0.70.

TELEPHONING BRAZIL
The code for dialling Brazil from abroad, after the access code (00 in most countries), is 55, followed by the area code you require (minus the initial 0).

TELEPHONING ABROAD
When making an international call from Brazil, dial 0+21, then the international country code you require followed by the area code (minus the initial 0 if there is one) and then the local number. International dialling codes are as follows: Australia 61, New Zealand 64, Republic of Ireland 353, South Africa 27, UK 44, US and Canada 1. For operator assistance, call 102.

Post
Sending post is surprisingly easy and efficient. Post offices can be found everywhere – just look for the ubiquitous blue-and-yellow insignia. Postcards to Europe and North America cost about R$1.50 to send. Count on items taking about a week to arrive at their destination.

Internet
Internet access is widespread across the country, but access speeds may be slower than you are used to, and costs may be greater. There will usually be at least one internet café in any town you visit.

CUSTOMS

English is spoken sporadically in Brazil and is usually limited to centres with many tourists or business visitors such as Rio and São Paulo. Even here, only staff who work in hotels and visitor hotspots have a good grasp of the language. Write the address of where you want to go on a slip of paper or bring a basic phrasebook with you to make life somewhat easier.

The nation is extremely macho, and strong elements of racism, sexism and homophobia continue to exist. Afro-Caribbean visitors may sometimes experience negative comments or challenging service in some locations. Mixed-race couples may also feel a certain degree of animosity, especially in cases where the male is 'white' and the female is of a darker skin tone, as she may be seen as a woman for hire.

Women should get used to catcalls and jeers from young men on the streets. A simple 'no' or a sharp look should put a stop to any unwelcome comments. Homosexuality is tolerated to a large extent by Brazilian locals. In fact, bisexuality is common among Brazilian men. Acts of violence are not unheard of, so any overt displays of same-sex affection on the streets should be avoided.

If you are using public transport or passing someone in the street, always give way to the elderly and mothers with children. Staying in your seat when a mother and child board a bus, for example, is frowned upon heavily in these parts.

When conversing, Brazilians can be very animated, using wild gesticulations – when both happy and sad. They may invade your personal space, but this is not intended to threaten you – unless you happen to be in an argument. If you *are* having an argument, slowly back away. However, if you back away during normal conversation, your companion may be offended – and causing offence is the very last thing you want to do, as tempers can flare hot and fast.

Service in shops and restaurants is very slow. In shops, most items are folded away in drawers, while in restaurants, waiters may not approach you for ages. This is not meant to annoy you; rather, locals look on shopping and eating as life's pleasures and prefer to extend the time both take. For them, life is about quality rather than speed.

Meals are eaten late and nightclubs and bars don't start going until the small hours of the morning. If you don't want to be the only person in the place, plan on waiting until well past midnight before leaving your hotel to begin the nightly revelries.

DRESS CODES

When travelling around Brazil, fit in with the locals and wear casual shorts and T-shirts – the skimpier the better. Brazilians also like to dress up for nights out on the town and when dining at expensive restaurants.

The only time you will need to dress conservatively is when you plan on visiting any monuments, museums, churches or government buildings. Here, you should wear shirts or blouses with long sleeves and skirts that go below the knee or trousers.

ELECTRICITY

The standard electrical current varies. In some places it is 110 V; in others it is 220 V. When you plug an appliance in, there is a good chance that you will blow the fuse, especially in more rural districts. Plugs are the same as you would find in continental Europe, with two round pins. Two-pin adaptors can be difficult to get hold of, so it is best that you pick one up before leaving home.

EMERGENCIES

EMERGENCY NUMBERS
Ambulance 193
Fire brigade 193
Police 190

Pharmacies are prevalent pretty much everywhere. You will not need a prescription for most drugs – pharmacists can even give injections on-site. In smaller communities, English-language skills may be limited.

Try to have any prescriptions you need or allergy notifications written down in Portuguese just in case. If you require a doctor or dentist, you are advised to consult your hotel reception. Failing that, your embassy or consulate should have information about English-speaking local doctors. Likewise, if you get into trouble with the police, have an accident, lose your passport or become a victim of crime, contact your embassy or consulate:

Australian Consulate ⓐ Veirano and Associates, Avenida Presidente Wilson 231, 23rd floor, Rio ⓣ 021 3824 4624 ⓦ www.brazil.embassy.gov.au

Canadian Consulate General ⓐ Avenida Atlântica 1130, 5th floor, Atlântica Business Center, Copacabana, Rio ⓣ 021 2543 3004 ⓦ www.canadainternational.gc.ca/brazil

UK Consulate-General ⓐ Praia do Flamengo 284, 2nd floor, Rio ⓣ 021 2555 9600 ⓦ www.britishembassy.gov.uk/brazil

US Consulate General ⓐ Avenida Presidente Wilson 147, Rio ⓣ 021 2292 7117 ⓦ http://brasilia.usembassy.gov

GETTING AROUND

Getting around Brazil can be challenging simply because of the vast distances involved. Low-cost airlines have done much to reduce the expense and you are well advised to check out the fares of the largest of them all – **Gol Airlines** ⓦ www.voegol.com.br – before finalising plans. Travelling by train isn't really an option. The country does have an extensive network of railways, but most are reserved for cargo trains. Suburban rail travel and trips around the south and Minas Gerais are easier to manage.

The bus and coach system in Brazil is extremely extensive and used widely. There are a number of firms that operate routes, but prices are set by the state and are standardised no matter what company you travel with. Fares are reasonable and comfort levels on long-distance trips are pleasant enough. Toilet facilities exist; you should try to request a seat within easy distance of the toilet for long journeys. For a luxury experience, book yourself on a *leito*, which is a premium coach that runs during the evening. Seats recline fully into beds and come complete with fresh sheets, curtained partitions and friendly attendants. *Leitos* need to be booked a few days in advance. All coaches depart from stations known as a *rodoviaria*, which are usually located on the city outskirts. All tickets need to be purchased at the station; your hotel reception can usually arrange this.

Car hire

Car hire is not advised in Brazil. Driving is erratic, break-ins are common and distances are long. If you have to hire a car, you will find that the vehicles are in excellent condition, but you should check for any signs of wear and tear before driving off, as otherwise you may be liable for a pre-existing dent when you return. Brazil also offers alcohol-powered cars, but these can be a pain to start and they break down frequently. The minimum age for renting an economy car is 21. For a larger car you'll need to be at least 25. Most rental companies will require you to be covered for both theft and collision damage. If they don't, you should get it anyway.

HEALTH, SAFETY & CRIME

Tap water is becoming increasingly safe to drink, although the taste may not be to your liking and some regions have better filtration and sanitation methods than others. Do not drink any water from lakes or rivers, as the country is not known for its commitment towards environmentalism. Most Brazilians prefer bottled mineral water, so it is probably best to do as the locals do.

Malaria is prevalent in northern Brazil and the Amazon (see page 113 for advice). Other diseases to watch out for include hepatitis A, cholera and Chagas's disease, which is transmitted through the faecal matter of a variety of beetles that live in the cracks of adobe walls in the Amazon. In the case of Chagas's, if you suspect you have a bite that is not transmitted by a mosquito, be sure to bathe it in alcohol. For hepatitis A and cholera, water is the transmitter, so you should be extremely suspicious of anything that has come close to suspect water.

Brazil is a country plagued by the scourge of HIV. So you would be well advised to use condoms to avoid the possibility of infection. Try to bring a stash from home, as Brazilian varieties are not as durable as those produced in North America or Europe. If in need, walk into a shop and ask for a *camiseta* ('little shirt').

Heatstroke is a common problem, so don't go anywhere without appropriate clothing and ample water supplies. A hat and plenty of sunscreen are vital.

Crime is a huge problem, especially after dark or on weekends in business districts. Be watchful at all times and leave your cash, cameras and expensive jewellery in the safe at your hotel. When travelling, take a taxi wherever you go, even if it is for just a short distance. Your hotel will warn you about particular areas to avoid.

When using public transport or walking on the street, carry your wallet in your front pocket, keep bags closed at all times, never leave valuables on the ground when you are seated at a table and always wear camera bags and handbags crossed over your chest.

MEDIA

Brazilian newspapers cover everything from international affairs to local fluff, but you wouldn't write home about the sparkling language or incisive commentary.

If you're wanting to stay in touch with the rest of the planet, you'll find a limited number of English-language publications, including *Time* and the *International Herald Tribune*, available in airports and premium hotel gift shops.

OPENING HOURS

Most shops and services open from 09.00–18.00 Monday–Friday with a two-hour lunch break somewhere in the middle. Markets can sometimes open and close earlier by a couple of hours. Cultural institutions usually follow the same hours as businesses and shops, but remain open at weekends, closing one day in the week instead (usually Monday). Banks open at 10.00 and remain open all day without a lunch break, but they stop exchanging foreign currency some time around 14.00.

RELIGION

Brazil is a Roman Catholic country. In fact, it lays claim to being the nation with the largest population of Roman Catholics in the world. Locals tend to be fairly devout, but church attendance is declining. Sundays remain an important family day. Evangelical churches are gaining in popularity in poorer communities. *Candomblé* – an Afro-Brazilian religion that draws its roots from the beliefs of slaves imported from among the Yoruba people of West Africa – is still practised in Salvador and Rio, where large black populations exist.

TIME DIFFERENCES

Brazil has three time zones. Zone one, which includes Rio, São Paulo, Salvador and all the major coastal resorts, is in the same time zone as New York City during the Northern Hemisphere's Daylight Saving between March and September. When the clocks go back in Europe and America, this time zone jumps two hours ahead of New York. Zone two includes the Pantanal, Manaus and the Amazon and is one hour behind Rio time. Zone three, which includes the state of Acre and the western Amazon, is two hours behind Rio.

TIPPING

A 10 per cent service charge is usually levied on most hotel and restaurant bills. If it has been included, there is no need to leave a further tip. With taxi drivers, just increase the fare to the nearest round figure and they'll be satisfied.

TOILETS

There are very few public toilet facilities anywhere in Brazil. The best approach is to use the toilet in a bar. You can usually walk straight in

without having to buy a drink. If the bar is empty, it is a matter of politeness to ask the bartender first. In restaurants there may be signs saying that toilets are only for the use of paying customers. Fast-food joints and department stores are other good options.

TRAVELLERS WITH DISABILITIES

For people with disabilities, Brazil is difficult to negotiate. While it is easy to go along the beach promenade, things get decidedly more challenging as you go inland. This is especially true in Rio and Salvador, where hilly topography and bad paving cause havoc for wheelchair users. The best thing to do is to ask someone who works at the location you are trying to enter if they can help you, as there may be ramps that can be placed over steps, for example. In museums, the ground floors are usually accessible, as are those in more modern galleries. Buses and trains, however, are completely wheelchair unfriendly.

The following sites should provide some helpful information:
Ⓦ www.access-able.com (general advice on worldwide travel)
Ⓦ www.sath.org (US-based site)
Ⓦ http://travel.guardian.co.uk/travellingwithdisabilities (UK site offering tips and links for disabled travellers)

ACKNOWLEDGEMENTS

We would like to thank all the photographers, picture libraries and organisations for the loan of the photographs reproduced in this book, to whom copyright in the photographs belongs:
DREAMSTIME R Arena (page 44), Artmann-Witte (pages 52, 60), A De Azevedo Negrão (page 91), E Sarles (page 38), Faberfoto (page 5), C Franck (pages 10–11, 21, 23, 109), Gabrieldome (page 94), M Gama (pages 71, 103), M Goldzweig (page 13), A Greco (page 58), Jeromaniac (page 107), P Loeb (page 81), Marcaux (page 48), A Moreaux (page 99), Mypix (pages 9, 35), A Nantel (page 27), Roza (page 115), B Ward (page 88).
GETTY IMAGES pages 65, 67, 90.
PICTURES COLOUR LIBRARY pages 30, 77.
WORLD PICTURES/PHOTOSHOT pages 17, 63, 84, 100, 105.

Project editor: Thomas Willsher
Layout: Paul Queripel
Copy editor: Anne McGregor
Proofreader: Rosalind Munro
Indexer: Marie Lorimer

Send your thoughts to
books@thomascook.com

- Found a beach bar, peaceful stretch of sand or must-see sight that we don't feature?

- Like to tip us off about any information that needs a little updating?

- Want to tell us what you love about this handy little guidebook and, more importantly, how we can make it even handier?

Then here's your chance to tell all! Send us ideas, discoveries and recommendations today and then look out for your valuable input in the next edition of this title.

Email to the above address or write to:
pocket guides Series Editor, Thomas Cook Publishing, PO Box 227, Unit 9, Coningsby Road, Peterborough PE3 8SB, UK.

Useful phrases

English	Portuguese	Approx pronunciation
BASICS		
Yes	Sim	*Seem*
No	Não	*Nown*
Please	Por favor	*Poor favohr*
Thank you	Obrigado/a	*Ohbreegahdoo/a*
Hello	Olá	*Ohlah*
Goodbye	Adeus	*Adayoosh*
Excuse me	Com licença	*Cong lisensah*
Sorry	Desculpe	*Dishkoolper*
That's okay	Está bem	*Istah bayn*
I don't speak Portuguese	Não sei falar Português	*Nown say falahr Portoogehsh*
Do you speak English?	Fala Inglês?	*Fahla eenglaysh?*
Good morning	Bom día	*Bohm deea*
Good afternoon	Boa tarde	*Boha tahrd*
Good evening	Boa noite	*Boha noyt*
My name is ...	Chamo-me ...	*Shamoo-mi ...*
NUMBERS		
One	Um	*Oong*
Two	Dois	*Doysh*
Three	Três	*Traysh*
Four	Quatro	*Kwahtroo*
Five	Cinco	*Seengkoo*
Six	Seis	*Saysh*
Seven	Sete	*Set*
Eight	Oito	*Oytoo*
Nine	Nove	*Nov*
Ten	Dez	*Desh*
Twenty	Vinte	*Veengt*
Fifty	Cinquenta	*Seengkwayngta*
One hundred	Cem	*Sayng*
SIGNS & NOTICES		
Airport	Aeroporto	*Aehrohportoo*
Railway station/ Platform	Estação de Caminho de Ferro/Linha	*Ishtasowng di Kamihnyo di Fehrroo/Leenya*
Smoking/ non-smoking	Fumadores/ Não fumadores	*Foomadohrsh/ Nown-foomadohrsh*
Toilets	Lavabos	*Lavahboosh*
Ladies/Gentlemen	Senhoras/Homens	*Sinyohrash/Omayngsh*